Praise for David Yetman

"Yetman's stories are about colorful characters.
Their images will stay with me."
—Goodreads

"Yetman's enthusiasm is infectious."
—*Quarterly Review of Biology*

"Yetman gives especially detailed accounts."
—*Science*

"[David Yetman] tickles our brain and gladdens our heart."
—Bill Broyles, co-author of *Last Water on the Devil's Highway*

"[Yetman's work offers] a key historical reference to
fellow scholars as well as the general reader."
—Kirstin Erickson, author of *Yaqui Homeland and Homeplace:
The Everyday Production of Ethnic Identity*

Praise for The Saguaro Cactus

"This is an excellent primer on a plant that defines our home and demands our respect and protection."

—Gregory McNamee, 2021 Southwest Books of the Year

"The perfect primer on this distinctive sentinel of the southwestern desert."

—*Journal of Arizona History*

"Anyone curious about the saguaro's history, ecology, and unparalleled adaptions to the desert's fierce climate will find ample answers to their questions here."

—Melissa L. Sevigny, author of *Under Desert Skies*

"*The Saguaro Cactus* is an extraordinary book written by extraordinary people."

—David E. Brown, Natural History Collections, Arizona State University

NATURAL LANDMARKS OF ARIZONA

The Southwest Center Series
Jeffrey M. Banister, Editor

NATURAL LANDMARKS

of

Arizona

DAVID YETMAN

**THE UNIVERSITY OF
ARIZONA PRESS**

TUCSON

The University of Arizona Press
www.uapress.arizona.edu

ISBN-13: 978-0-8165-4245-1 (paperback)

Cover design by Leigh McDonald
Cover photograph of Lost Dutchman State Park by Alex/Unsplash
Designed and typeset by Leigh McDonald in Apollo 10.25/15 and Ganache (display)

The maps on pp. 9 and 13 are by Paul Mirocha.

Library of Congress Cataloging-in-Publication Data
Names: Yetman, David, 1941– author.
Title: Natural landmarks of Arizona / David Yetman.
Other titles: Southwest Center series.
Description: Tucson : The University of Arizona Press, 2021. | Series: Southwest Center series
    | Includes index.
Identifiers: LCCN 2021004383 | ISBN 9780816542451 (paperback)
Subjects: LCSH: Mountains—Arizona. | Geology, Structural—Arizona. | Arizona—Descrip-
    tion and travel.
Classification: LCC F817.A16 Y48 2021 | DDC 917.9104—dc23
LC record available at https://lccn.loc.gov/2021004383

Printed in the United States of America
♾ This paper meets the requirements of ANSI/NISO Z39.48-1992 (Permanence of Paper).

For my brother Richard Yetman,
who tugged and guided me into geology

Contents

NATURAL LANDMARKS OF ARIZONA

Why Landmarks?

Landmarks as Locators

This book is about landmarks, parts of the earth that intrude into the Arizona horizon. They are irregularities, reminders that the earth we live on is not flat, a fact so obvious, yet so ignored. Projections of rock rise from the ground into the sky. They orient us. They locate us. They are steadfast through generations. They define where we live and where we are, though we may not reckon as much. They are the monuments that rescue us from geographical monotony. Those who have experienced only flatlands and steppes—the Midwest prairies, Florida, south Texas—may not understand, but one visit to the desert Southwest can rectify that.

My fascination with landmarks began at Duncan, Arizona, a small town that has never received widespread acclaim for the majesty of its landscapes. For me, however, its natural monuments were bewitching and formative. Duncan is an agrarian town of about eight hundred souls, situated on the south bank of the Gila River near the state line with New Mexico. I moved there with my family as a lad from rural New Jersey. For some reason I felt an inordinate need to identify landmarks in this new land and learn their names. From

Duncan and its valley rise an array of prominences especially impressive for a young New Jersey transplant. Old-timers in the Duncan Valley taught me the names: Steeple Rock, Mount Royal, Vanderbilt, Apache Box, Ash Peak, Black Hills, Mulligan Peak, and Caneastor, most of them lying in New Mexico north and east of the Gila River. Far in the distance to the west towered Mount Graham, routinely visible from atop the mesa above the town. For me, learning their names was almost as good as climbing them. Almost. I did manage to climb most of them. All of these peaks were grand beyond anything I had experienced in the gentle tree-covered landscape of New Jersey. In that ancient terrain, Cushetunk Mountain was the regional prominence, its unassuming, forested summit 450 feet above its base. In Duncan, it would hardly have merited a name. Duncan has mountains nearby that rise more than 2,500 feet from their bases. Mount Graham, forty-some miles to the west, rises 8,000 feet from bottom to top. These were real mountains. Over time I was inclined to find out about their history and, much later, understand what forces caused them to be there. More than sixty years later, those landmarks and my recollection of them over the years still help define my stay in that small town and that formative part of my life.

This book features natural monuments, those features of Arizona's landscape that stand out as they are and as they were before the arrival of humans. They rise from the earth's surface in a manner that we cannot help but notice, though we may pay little attention to them and may even ignore them. We may take them for granted, but they influence who we are and where we are far more than most of us acknowledge.

In the mid-1960s, a decade after I arrived in Duncan, the world of structural geology was transformed—shaken, electrified—by a new theory, now an established fact: plate tectonics. The new scientific paradigm described the earth's crust as a composite of massive, floating plates that move independently of each other and from time to time collide, while at other times rifting apart and breaking off. The

Landmarks seen from the Duncan Valley, looking to the northeast. Left to right: Vanderbilt, Mount Royal, Steeple Rock. All three are of volcanic origin.

discovery arose from multiple sources and is credited to multiple discoverers, but almost instantly the revolution drew a phalanx of researchers energized by the new model (and a stern group of resolute and stubborn opponents). When I was young, geologists had detailed maps of terrain, rocks, peneplains, thrust belts, and erosion surfaces. Field geologists were a hardy breed, weathered by constant exposure to the elements, intimately familiar with rocks and their place in geological history. They assembled sophisticated descriptions and cross sections of the landscapes and the rocks that formed them, and many were brilliant analysts. They determined the age of rocks based on their relationship to fossil-bearing strata. They composed geologic maps of astonishing detail, with accuracy unsurpassed even now. One such geologist, David Love, single-handedly created the geologic map of Wyoming. Thirty years later, he equally single-handedly revised it. It remains the authoritative document for the state.

But geniuses though they might have been, those earlier scientists had only vague and confusing explanations for the existence of these landforms and mountain ranges, volcanoes, and irregular terrain. They had difficulty explaining why landscapes weren't simply flat. Where landmarks were clearly of volcanic origin, field observations provided the geologists with precise evidence of the nature and origin of the volcanism and volcanics, but they were helpless to explain why the volcanism was there in the first place.* How some mountain ranges and associated valleys came to be, their relationships to others, and the precise time scale in which it all happened were enshrouded in mystery. An instructive example comes from a discussion of the origin of diastrophism—mountain building—in an excellent textbook from 1966: "Some kind of very slow thermal convection—the rise of relatively warm columns and sinking of relatively cool ones—is a favored hypothesis for the ultimate cause of diastrophism."† For the most part, geologists prior to the 1960s could not explain why the earth is not everywhere flat, at least more or less flat. German geophysicist Alfred Wegener had proposed in 1912 that continents drifted, moving around as though floating and frequently (over deep time) bumping into each other. His theory was ridiculed,

---

* Instructive examples of superb geology written during the early emergence of plate tectonics, but not reliant on the theory, include Andrew Shride, *Younger Precambrian Geology in Southern Arizona* (Geological Survey Professional Paper 566, U.S. Government Printing Office, 1967), and an authoritative account of the geology of the Colorado Plateau written without consideration of plate tectonics, *The Colorado Plateau: A Geological History* (University of New Mexico Press, 2000), by Donald Baars. Baars was a consulting geologist irritated by what he saw as the unwarranted enthusiasm of a new generation of glib geologists spouting plate tectonic jargon. He expressed indignation about what he considered their lack of field experience and their overconfidence and was skeptical of the accuracy and usefulness of the new theory. A startling contrast, however, is a work about geology of the Southwest based entirely on plate tectonics, Scott Baldridge's *Geology of the American Southwest* (Cambridge University Press, 2004).

† John Shelton, *Geology Illustrated* (San Francisco: W. H. Freeman, 1966), 423.

and he was roundly denounced by his geologist peers.[‡] But he was mostly right.

Within a decade of its formulation, plate tectonics theory changed our understanding of landscape formation. Researchers identified the deep forces and plate movements that helped explain the earth's surface features and the evolution of landscapes. Mountains were the result of plate collisions. Valleys were produced by separating blocks as plates pulled apart. A bumper sticker from that time read "Fight Continental Drift." At roughly the same time, new techniques for determining the age of rocks emerged, now called radiometric dating. These procedures allowed researchers to plunge into deep time and provide increasingly accurate estimates of the age of rocks.[§] These discoveries gave a new and expanded importance to a technological accomplishment: Beginning in the 1950s deep drilling for minerals and fossil fuels to depths greater than 10,000 feet produced cores that revealed the earth's composition to that depth. When the cores were analyzed and laid side by side, they revealed what lay beneath the surface of rocks and the layers below, underneath the canyons, mountains, and flatlands—and gave clues to their origins. They detailed the innards of the earth's crust at depths profoundly greater than previously possible. They gave rise to precise graphs of the earth below its surface. It was as though the earth was a colossal layer cake covered by thick icing, and the drilling divulged the nature of the layers hidden beneath that icing. One core showed

---

[‡] In the mid-nineteenth century French paleontologist (and future celebrated Harvard professor) Jean Louis Agassiz proclaimed that European landscapes had been shaped by glaciers that had long since retreated or vanished. He was ridiculed and ostracized, though ultimately vindicated in his own lifetime. In turn, Agassiz ridiculed Darwin's work on evolution.

[§] Not all rocks are amenable to the dating techniques. Sandstone defies the technology, and metamorphic rocks may be resistant to precise measurement of age.

little, but tens, hundreds of cores compared side by side gave a picture of the underground and its history.

By the early 1970s, geologists by the thousands were using the new tectonics model along with dating technology, incorporating information from those legions of cores brought up from the bowels of the deep to explain the visible and invisible structure of the earth's crust. And this combination of sources made the origin and nature of landmarks around us more intelligible. Some more traditional geologists lamented the new theory of plate tectonics as an excuse for younger geologists to spend less time in the field. But the revolution in geology was nearly as dramatic as Darwin's explanation of evolution or Einstein's theories of the cosmos. New explanations and models for landforms continue to emerge as scientists gain a deeper understanding of the face and basement of the earth. The picture becomes clearer—but very slowly and by painfully tiny bits.

Why Arizona?

For simplicity and to make this book manageable, I have limited its scope to Arizona. This state has been my home since the mid-1950s, and parts of it are branded into my consciousness. Since my arrival in Arizona, I have lived for at least two years in Duncan, Prescott, Mesa, the Chiricahua Mountains, and Tucson. Except for eighteen months of college in California, I have lived nowhere else since that time. Those locales have provided me with a grand sampling of the state's landscapes. I had ample but uncomprehending exposure to granites more than 1.4 *billion* years old in Prescott. Prescottonians celebrated the towering presence of Thumb Butte, unaware, as I was, that the surrounding granite was one hundred times older than that lava flow. I also lived among youthful rhyolites (26 million years old) in the Chiricahuas, and climbed among the 1.4-billion-year-old

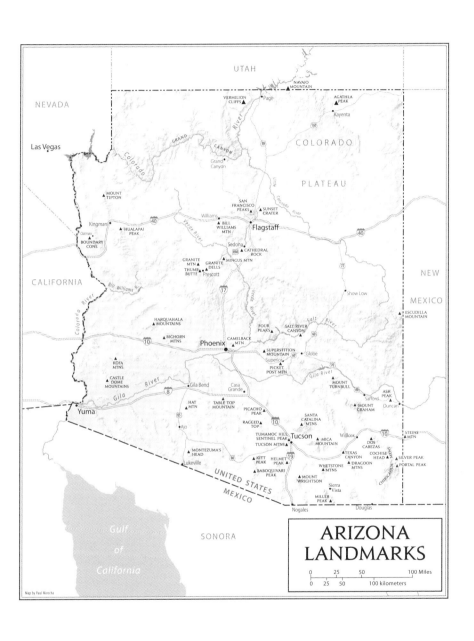

ARIZONA LANDMARKS

granites of the Santa Catalina Mountains north of Tucson. I saw snow on the 1.7-billion-year-old quartzite of Four Peaks, east of Mesa.

I would love to include landmarks from elsewhere in the Southwest—western New Mexico, southeastern Utah, and southwestern Colorado—but those regions have plenty of advocates and will have to get their just desserts elsewhere. Within Arizona's border lie an abundance of natural landmarks equal to any comparable part of the United States. This is no chauvinistic boast but rather a demonstration of how geology and climate combine to identify a region. Arizona is mostly mountainous and arid, and that combination produces a bounty of landmarks. With that abundance of visible markers comes a wealth of cultural involvement in the landscape. Peoples for hundreds of generations before us have been subject to the power of those landmarks, have named them, fought over them, exploited them, and revered them. Landscapes of the Americas have penetrated human consciousness for well over 10,000 years.

Arizona's landmarks have come and gone over time. A geologist once told me that mountain ranges typically rise from the plains and are leveled back to them in about 200 million years. But mountains seldom simply sit passively as they rise and erode. Constant tectonic movement drops some ranges and raises others, stretches many, compresses others, and tilts an impressive number of them. Balloonings of magma—batholiths and plutons—from many kilometers below the surface may raise huge tracts of land. They may float ancient rock up into the visible landscape hundreds of millions of years after it was initially formed and was subsequently buried under sediments or belts of rock. Elevation to the surface of rock once buried kilometers deep is not unusual. A marvelous example is Four Peaks in the Mazatzal Range, a massive chunk of 1.7-billion-year-old quartzite raised or perhaps floated to the surface from deep underground only a few hundred million years ago. The granite on which it rests is nearly a billion years *younger* than the quartzite—the older rock towering over younger rock. It, too, was raised to the surface by tectonic activity—a continental-sized bulldozer—and revealed by erosion.

Periods of mountain building have created enormous ranges and massive volcanoes in the Southwest, many of which have been beaten and ground down by wind, rain, ice, and heat of the sun and the rising and falling of the earth's crust. Around 300 million years ago (MYA), tectonic forces pushed up a massive range northeast of Arizona now known as the Ancestral Rockies. Erosion and plate movements have beveled that army of mountains, softened and largely obliterated them from the landscape, tearing apart their substance and transporting their colossal amounts of rock to sites below— basins, valleys, canyons, and oceans—often to be recycled as other rock formations. The Rockies rose once again in the last 80 million years or so during the Laramide orogeny. Once again they are being dismantled, even as some of the mountains continue to rise.

Arizona is less dramatic geologically than it would have appeared beginning roughly a half million years ago. At that time an enormous volcano dominated the landscape: the San Francisco Peaks, which at that time was but one mountain. It reached nearly 16,000 feet in elevation, probably higher than any other peak in the lower forty-eight states. This stratovolcano either blew off its top or, more likely, lost its upper 3,000 feet or so in one or several colossal landslides. And nearly all our landmarks have spent the last two million years being eroded and reduced in size, with only occasional mountain building going on. Unlike the Grand Teton Mountains in Wyoming and some of the Rocky Mountains of Colorado, which are still growing, most of our monuments are steadily shrinking, but very, very slowly from a human perspective. As they are ground, dissolved, and whittled away, much of their losses accumulate at their bases, raising the elevation at the bottom even as the top lowers. Geologists tell me that we can take some comfort in the realization that for every ten inches that are eroded away, the mountain mass rises nine inches in response to the natural elasticity of crust beneath them as it rebounds from the lightened load. It is possible that the removal, the sliding away, of some 30 MYA of the Tucson Mountain mass from atop what are now the Santa Catalina and Rincon Mountains relieved the plutons emplaced beneath of a gargantuan burden. They had been lying below, some for over a billion years, others only around 50 million years. Freed from the enormous overburden and powered by rising magma, they rose from perhaps seven miles deep to nearly two miles above sea level.

Arizona Physiographic Provinces

Geologists have divided Arizona into three geological provinces: From northeast to southwest, the first is the Colorado Plateau, which occupies the northeastern third of the state. Second is the Transition Zone, a diagonal northwest-to-southeast wedge roughly eighty miles wide at the southeast corner that pinches out in the northwestern part of the state. It more or less parallels the edge of the Colorado Plateau and is described as a transition from the lofty plateau to the comparatively low deserts. Third is the Basin and Range Province that covers the southwestern half of the state. The boundary between the Transition Zone and Basin and Range is not sharply defined, but the division provides a most useful tool for understanding the state's topography and, as a result, the structure of many of the monuments.

The Colorado Plateau is most recognizable for its many colorful strata, mostly horizontal layers laid out in chronological order, that cover the entire region. The layers are evident anywhere erosion has removed some materials but left more resistant rock behind, or where watercourses have gouged away large chunks and exposed what is beneath the surface, or where old faults or younger compressions have caused wrinkles or folds in the once-horizontal layers. The plateau's innards are strikingly revealed in the Grand

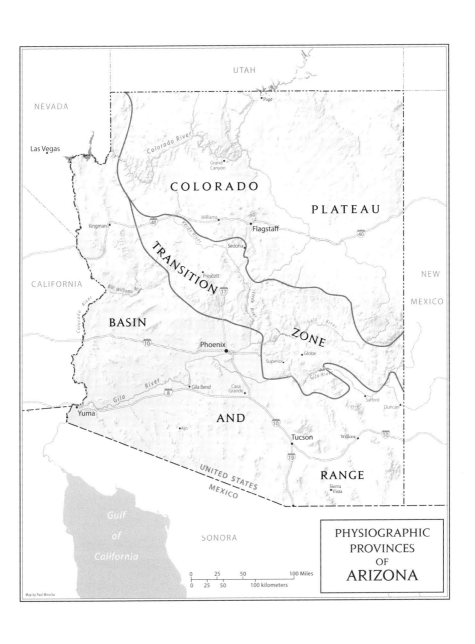

UTAH

NEVADA

Las Vegas

• Page

Colorado River

COLORADO

Grand
Canyon

Kingman

Williams

PLATEAU

Flagstaff

40

Verde River

Sedona

TRANSITION

Prescott

17

NEW

CALIFORNIA

Bill Williams R.

Colorado River

BASIN

10

Verde River

Salt River

ZONE

MEXICO

Phoenix

Superior

Globe

Gila River

Gila River

8

Gila Bend

Casa
Grande

Safford

Duncan

Yuma

AND

Ajo

10

RANGE

UNITED STATES

10

Tucson

Willcox

MEXICO

19

Sierra
Vista

Gulf

of

California

SONORA

0   25   50   100 Miles

0   25   50   100 kilometers

PHYSIOGRAPHIC
PROVINCES
OF
ARIZONA

Map by Paul Mirocha

Canyon, a sensational boon to the geologist, as it presents a diorama of Arizona's geological history from about 1.8 billion years ago to the present, with only a few gaps or unconformities in the record (though at one point the gap is more than one billion years). The state's most active volcanoes are located within the plateau—the Navajo, San Francisco, Springerville, Uinkaret, and White Mountains volcanic fields and the Hopi Buttes are all conspicuous features of volcanic activity within the mid-Tertiary period, roughly the last 30 million years. Some activity is as recent as 900 years ago. But apart from the volcanoes, the Colorado Plateau is a rather stable place, where the oldest visible rocks (with only a few exceptions) derive from the Paleozoic and Mesozoic eras, from 541 million years or so ago to some 66 million years ago. Precambrian rocks, those more than 541 million years old, can be seen only in remote sections of the bottom of the Grand Canyon. The plateau extends well into southeastern Utah, southwestern Colorado, and northwestern New Mexico. It ends abruptly at the Mogollon Rim in the south and the Grand Wash Cliffs at the western limits of the Grand Canyon.

The Colorado Plateau is also the easiest province to study, geologically speaking. The strata are well laid out, though considerable regional variations complicate the picture. Some formations pinch out in one direction and expand in another, usually a reflection of ancient seas that encroached and receded from various directions over vast expanses of time. The colorful Schnebly Hill Formation, which forms the backdrop for Sedona and Oak Creek Canyon, is absent from the Grand Canyon. It was formed near the edge of an ancient sea that never reached farther north. In parts of the plateau, entire eras have been eroded away, while others have been buried. Vast portions have been uplifted, others downdropped. Especially in parts of northern Arizona and southern Utah, slabs of rock a hundred miles long have been tilted into the air or forced downward, producing what are known as folds and hogbacks. The area is shot through with monoclines, anticlines, and synclines. In general, though, formations lie one on top of another in order of decreasing age (though at times one must fuss around a bit to determine what lies on top and what lies at the bottom). Geologically speaking, it is one of our hemisphere's neatest layouts. Its handiness is enhanced by its general aridity.

Not so with the Transition Zone, nor with Basin and Range. Their layout is usually far from neat. In both provinces, the country rock has been faulted, thrusted, twisted, tilted, folded, broken, and eroded in so many ways that it has taken experts decades to untangle the geological history. Challenges remain.

The Transition Zone (also known as the Central Mountain Zone) is a band situated roughly between the Mogollon Rim, a dramatic cliff face that demarks the edge of the Colorado Plateau, and the desert Southwest. It is in this province that the effects of plate tectonics over the last billion and a half years are most evident and the oldest rocks in the state are most frequently exposed, some of them dating to more than 1.7 billion years ago. The granite boulders around Prescott are a billion years older than anything visible on the surface of the Colorado Plateau. The zone is highly mountainous, replete with rugged, tortured landscapes, massive faults, highly dissected mountain ranges, and river courses and basins that reflect a battle of underlying tectonic plates. Highways in the Transition Zone seldom have long stretches of straightaways. Where the zone's southern margin should be located is the object of discussion among geologists. Most agree that it ends just north of Kingman. Beyond that, the Colorado Plateau ends at the Grand Wash Cliffs and Basin and Range begins immediately to the west.

The Basin and Range Province is largely a product of extensional stretching (pulling apart) that began some 15–17 MYA, perhaps earlier. Since that time, the crust of the earth has been pulled westward and northwestward, producing massive tears in the surface. As a result of the rifting, large blocks have broken off. Some of these have risen, while others immediately adjacent have fallen, leaving a series of alternating mountains and valleys in the southern and western portions of the state. The mountain ranges are for the most part oriented from the southeast to the northwest, notable for the predictability of valleys that separate the more or less parallel ranges. While the ages of the rocks in these ranges vary enormously (the rock of the summit of Mount Graham is roughly 1.7 billion years old, while that of Chiricahua Peak is about 26 million years old), Basin and Range is also home to entire landscapes of colossal volcanic activity, much of it occurring between 30 and 15 MYA. Here and there, rocks around 1.7 billion years old are exposed. In other ranges identified as metamorphic core complexes, such as the Santa Catalina Mountains, uplift has exposed rocks more than 1.4 billion years old.

I must apologize to the reader for resorting to geology and its complex terminology for explanations of how some landmarks came to be. But only by understanding basic geological forces can we appreciate why landmarks are where they are and demystify their arrival and appearance on the landscapes. Agathla, Monument Valley, Picacho Peak, the San Francisco Peaks—all owe their prominence to geological activities peculiar to or well exemplified in the Southwest. The ages of the rock in Southwest monuments range from less than one thousand years old (Sunset Crater) to more than 1.7 million times that old: 1.7 billion years, such as Four Peaks, the lower slopes of Dos Cabezas, and the summit of Mount Graham. Elves Chasm gneiss at the bottom of western reaches of the Grand Canyon has been estimated to be 1.84 billion years old.

What disorients most of us without formal geological training is grappling with time. The vastness of the past is upsetting and incomprehensible on the face of it. Creationist explanations—the earth is roughly 6,000 years old and was created by God in a rapid time span—are far more reassuring to most human psyches, given the short length of the human life span, but they offer no insight into our landscapes and are empirically false. The roughly two million years since the Pleistocene epoch began—the most recent round of ice age advances and retreats—seems like an unfathomably long period, yet the Pleistocene is but a single week in a lifetime when compared with the 4.5 billion years since the earth's geological history began. The roughly five-million-year period needed for the Colorado River to carve out the Grand Canyon occupies barely more than one-thousandth of the earth's age, one-tenth of one percent. Vertebrates have been around less than 15 percent of the planet's past, humans less than one-tenth of one percent. The landmarks that we see are tiny chunks of the past, most of them appearing in geologically recent times. In Arizona, only a few monuments, constructed from the most durable of rock, such as Four Peaks, the summit of Mount Graham, and the granites in the vicinity of Prescott, can truly be said to have withstood the test of time.

A related impediment to our acceptance of deep time is the excruciatingly slow (from our perspective) changes of the geological landscape. We can view the same landscape over a lifetime and fail to detect even the slightest alteration. Apart from volcanoes, earthquake displacements, and landslides, we have little personal evidence of the movement of tectonic plates, erosion of deep canyons, or uplift and leveling of mountains. Major tectonic plates may move rapidly from a geological standpoint, but without sophisticated satellite and delicate terrestrial measurements, we would not even be aware of them or the fact that they move. Thanks to the understanding of plate tectonics and precise measuring techniques, geologists know that the Baja California Peninsula, powered by the San Andreas Fault and the plate and landmass of which it is a part, is moving toward the northwest at about five centimeters a year, a velocity geologists view as breathtakingly fast. Over a human lifetime of seventy years, that amounts to about four meters, twelve feet, unimaginably slow for a human psyche to detect. Over a million years, however, it amounts to about 50 kilometers, 31 miles. Over the last five million years, from the beginning of the Pliocene to the present, the peninsula has moved 250 kilometers, 160 miles, relative to the mainland of Mexico. To the northwest during that time, successive earthquakes along the San Andreas Fault have managed to raise the San Bernardino Mountains of southern California more than two miles into the sky. But our experience, our lifetime of observations, is allotted only a microscopic portion of that change. The whole idea seems to defy reason. For those unaccepting of scientific pronouncements, deep geology is a tough sell.

A Simple Chronology of Arizona's Recent Geological History

The Southwest and Arizona, along with most of the western United States, have a recent history (the last 80 million years or so) of intense plate tectonic activity and volcanoes associated with plate movements. Most (but not all) of our southwestern mountains—that is, visible geological features—derived their present shape from three periods of mountain building contained in that brief (geologically speaking) period. The oldest of geological activities that have shaped most of what we see is the Laramide orogeny, the great mountain-building period from roughly 80 MYA to between 35 and 50 MYA. That period of epically slow plate warfare began when one tectonic plate, the Farallon, located beneath what is now the Pacific Ocean, dived eastward under another plate, the North American, at an increasingly low angle, somewhere considerably east of what is now the West Coast, and wrought havoc at the surface; it kept pushing and shoving until its far western edge, a spreading center—a site where the earth's surface was rifting apart—was consumed at the edge of the North American Plate, like the tail of a snake disappearing down a rodent hole. The clash of plate and plate (the heavier Farallon was subducted, that is, burrowed, or more accurately, tunneled under the more buoyant North American Plate and pulled the rest of the plate along with it) gave rise to stupendous rearranging of the western landscape, producing volcanic activity and pushing up the Rocky Mountains. Some geologists believe that about 60 MYA Laramide forces initiated the uplift of the Colorado Plateau. The force of the plate moving eastward raised the plateau without greatly altering its surface, through which the Colorado River has, in the last 5 million years (or perhaps less), carved out the Grand Canyon. The Laramide also formed and deformed landscapes throughout the West. The Rockies reach their southern limit in central or northern New Mexico, but the overall effects of Laramide tectonic movement extend far beyond them, well into southern Arizona and far south into Mexico. In general, the Laramide reactivated every existing fault and rearranged the entire landscape of the western United States. This massive geological shakeup gave us the Rocky Mountains, though it has left little in the way of landmarks in Arizona. The Laramide was responsible for uplifts of the land and produced movements—clashes—among enormous expanses of rock already ancient. It raised gigantic mountains and opened enormous abysses, drove vast layers of rock over, under, and through other layers, pushing some along, elevating some, depressing others, crumpling, bending, and breaking whole landscapes in the process. In general, the Laramide orogeny established high-elevation plateaus throughout much of the western United States and set things in motion for later geological processes that are still going on. Furthermore, the effects of the plate clash reached as far east as southwestern South Dakota, where it gave rise to the Black Hills.

Perhaps more important in forming landmarks in the Southwest—often the most visibly striking landmarks—is our rich and powerful volcanic tradition, a second source of our geological markers. During the last 34 million years or so, the region between the Rio Grande rift zone in New Mexico and the Colorado River in western Arizona, along with the Snake-Columbia River region of the northwestern United States, has been one of the most volcanically active on Earth, and that, more than any other terrestrial activity, has given rise to our current landscape. Arizona alone has twenty different lava fields from this period, each with its own history and source of volcanic material and its often highly individual results. The San Francisco Peaks, Mount Baldy in the White Mountains, and the Superstition Mountains at the eastern end of the Salt River Valley are three strikingly different examples of Arizona's volcanic heritage. The Chiricahua Mountains in southeastern Arizona and the Kofas near Yuma are both volcanic in their origins and not far apart in age. From far above, viewers from space can see the Jémez lineament, a nearly straight line of volcanic action cutting a diagonal from east-central Arizona northeast across northern New Mexico. The Mexican Sierra Pinacate, whose northern edges lie in southwestern Arizona, contains lava flows laid down within the last 12,000 years. And yes, the Pinacate region is still volcanically active.

Volcanic landscapes are often more visible in the Southwest than elsewhere due to skimpy vegetation cover in our drier climate. Lavas, volcanic tuff, and ash deposits endure longer and are less liable to concealment here than in wetter climes. Even so, over the many millions of years since the volcanic forms appeared, water and wind have worked their will, and the Southwest landscape is replete with jagged remnants of flows, domes, and diatremes buried, exhumed, tilted, and thus altered by erosive forces over the last 30 million years. These are in addition to a multitude of exposed volcanic rocks of even greater age. The chaotic Tucson Mountains, for example, are made up mostly of volcanic rock more than 70 million years old that arrived at the surface, possibly while the range was still atop what are now the Santa Catalina Mountains.

Thirdly, many landmarks are the result of extensional faulting, that is, huge breaks in the surface crust that developed as the landscape was stretched west/northwestward in the geological province known as Basin and Range in Arizona and the Rio Grande Rift in New Mexico. Basin and Range is the more recent geological phenomenon and responsible for the proliferation of landmarks in the desert Southwest, especially in the southern and western portions. Roughly

The Crater Range, north of Ajo, Arizona. The rock formations are dikes of rhyolite lava, roughly 17 million years of age.

17 MYA, large crustal portions of the western United States and northwestern Mexico underwent stretching from the west/northwest, when part of the Pacific Plate that had been crashing toward the North American Plate changed direction in its movement from east to northwest. Over those millions of years, the Sierra Nevada in California has migrated nearly 180 miles to the west of Salt Lake City, Utah, stretching out the entire landscape between the two places as it has pulled away. The extensional pulling apart caused the entire stretched region to subside, while the more durable Colorado Plateau remained largely unaffected, giving the incorrect impression that the plateau had risen. The enormous tension on the crust as the region was pulled and stretched toward the west resulted in the thinning and tearing of the upper part of the earth's crust similar to a slice of pizza being pulled from an entire pie. Something had to give. Or, we should say, a lot of things had to give. Large sections or blocks of crust broke apart. Some of these immense blocks rose, as if bouncing up, while others on either side fell into the resulting

void, thus creating mountains with intervening valleys (horsts and grabens—sometimes half-grabens, that is, a graben tilted to one side). Geological forces have shifted the blocks on their centers of gravity, tilting them, raising parts, burying others, exalting and debasing, concealing some of the parts miles beneath the surface, exhuming others from equal depths and elevating them skyward. Landmarks such as Mount Graham in Arizona's Pinaleño Mountains, Baboquivari Peak, the Hualapai Mountains, Mount Wrightson in the Santa Rita Mountains, and Neumann Peak in the Picacho Mountains are a result of that process, called block faulting. Gravity and erosion immediately began tearing down the rising blocks, ripping chunks away, filling the voids, which became (often fertile) valleys with sediments thousands of feet deep that have proved ideal for storing water that poured into the basins over millions of years. In the northern reaches of the Basin and Range Province the stretching continues, as the San Andreas Fault chugs along toward the northwest, pulling Baja California with it, deepening California's Salton Sea, lengthening the distance between Salt Lake City and Reno, Nevada, and endangering the lives and property of many millions of residents in its area of influence, mostly California. Death Valley may be a crack in the earth that represents the boundary between the new California and the old continent as a new gulf opens. In a few thousand years, a structural geologist warned me, the Salton Sea will be lower than Death Valley, and the Gulf of California will have rushed in to fill the depths. Cracks resulting from the stretching also have produced weaknesses in the crust, creating an easier route for magma to reach the surface. This is graphically evident in the Uinkaret volcanic field northwest of the Grand Canyon, where in the last million years or so magma has emerged from the deep through cracks that appear as the surface pulls away from the Colorado Plateau. Through those cracks rivers of lava flowed and poured over the north rim into the Grand Canyon, piling up into dams on at least seventeen occasions, one of which created a lake that extended three hundred miles northeast into what is now Utah. Cracking, that is, Basin and Range faulting, was also responsible for a major earthquake in 1887 that originated in Mexico just south of Douglas, Arizona. Probably a jarring 7.5 on the Richter scale, it destroyed several towns in Mexico and the mining boomtown of Charleston near present-day Sierra Vista, Arizona. Charleston never recovered. Sierra Vista and Fort Huachuca, beware.

The Rio Grande region of New Mexico and southern Colorado began to tear apart along the rift zone long before Basin and Range, beginning about 30 MYA as the north-south crack was created. The two sides were rendered asunder and the Rio Grande's course was created, or at least modified. The formations that derived from the southern portion of the rift, from near Las Cruces north to Truth or Consequences or thereabouts, are older than, but difficult to distinguish from, the Basin and Range Province. As the western portion of the rift was tugged westward (the eastern portion appears to have been more securely attached to its tectonic foundation), volcanism derived from weakening of the crust resulted in massive exhalations of lava and ash and the formation of volcanic necks, craters, calderas, and stratovolcanoes, much of which are found in what is known as the Datil-Mogollon volcanic field. That cauldron extends from the Organ Mountains near Las Cruces to the White Mountains in Arizona and well north. Escudilla Mountain is part of that volcanic chain. In New Mexico's Bootheel and extreme southeastern Arizona, at least nine massive calderas appeared on the landscape between 33 MYA and 26 MYA. Two of them formed the Chiricahua Mountains.

In terms of visible reminders of volcanism, no other place in Arizona can match the Black Mountains of the northwestern part of the state. The seventy-five-mile-long range, our state's longest, is a sensational diorama of cataclysmic volcanic activity of the Miocene, probably about 18 MYA. A spectacular remnant identifies the semi-ghost town of Oatman. Two friends of mine a generation older grew up there, part of a family of miners. Though they moved away to attend college, never to return, they must have had imprinted in

Elephant Tooth, Oatman. It towers above the town's main and only street.

their minds and consciousness the image of Elephant Tooth, a whitish rhyolite volcanic neck jutting immediately above the town and commanding the attention of all who live there.

While geological unrest has been exalting some landmarks, weather has been whittling away at all of them. Arizona, however, is in general the driest state of the United States: the region as a whole is mostly semiarid or arid. The wettest location is probably somewhere high in the San Francisco Peaks, where total annual rainfall averages about thirty inches, roughly the same as Minneapolis, historically (but less so now) much of it in snowfall. That quantity of precipitation, however, is confined to a tiny area at elevations over 10,000 feet. The reality of the rest of the state is stark: Tucson averages just under twelve inches of precipitation a year. Phoenix averages around seven inches. Yuma and the lower Colorado River region receive only three inches. That area occupies many thousands of square miles. The higher temperatures toward the southwestern portion of the region increase rates of evaporation and add to the effects of aridity. Usually, the drier the climate, the less erosion affects the landscape, the starker the geology, and the more spectacular are the rocky landscapes. Mountains of extreme southwestern Arizona have a notable starkness, a sharpness that reflects the scarceness of erosion by water. Their bases lack the concealing and softening effects of large alluvial fans or accumulations of sediments that ease the approach to mountains' bases. Apart from the higher mountains and plateaus, rainfall throughout the Southwest is insufficient to provide forest cover—and generally precludes widespread dryland agriculture.

One of the first things I learned about the Southwest was that nothing on the landscape is hidden—well, at least far less is hidden than in northwestern New Jersey. Field geologists love the Southwest partly because the rock that forms the landscapes is easily observable nearly everywhere. Exposed rocks are not confined to roadcuts, as they tend to be in wetter climates, and the rock of the mountains is usually in full display. When roadcuts appear, they often remain barren of vegetation for decades. Unlike in the rest of the country, mountains and hills at their lower elevations are for the most part undisguised by vegetation, and the clarity of the air (unless tainted by pollutants and haze from forest fires) admits of views of distant landmarks. At the same time, scant rainfall means that erosion from rain, though always at work, has been slower to soften and round off the landscape, to dissolve and wash off the roughness of rock. Moss, vine, and shrub disguise, conceal, obscure, and slowly dissolve and disintegrate the rocks, rises, hills, and peaks they cover. The Southwest is not kind to or tolerant of these softeners. Lichens, abundant in arid lands, attach to rock, but they pick away at it and digest it at a leisurely pace. In the hotter and drier portions of the Southwest a phenomenon called desert varnish covers exposed stones and durable rock faces and helps preserve rock from erosion. Sheer sandstone cliffs and basaltic lava, which abound in the Southwest, are especially receptive to desert varnish.

The varnish also presents a canvas on which artists may etch their impressions. Europe's well-preserved ancient art was largely confined to painting in dry caves, but the Southwest has numerous varnished surfaces inviting artistic enhancement by incision rather than painting. For thousands of years, natives have left their creations etched in desert varnish for the public to behold. Southwestern landscapes are often stark reminders of defiance of the forces of erosion.

Finally, landmarks in Arizona are usually visible, both from close by and from afar. Sensational prominences elsewhere that tower over the countryside, such as Mount Hood in Oregon, Mount Rainier in Washington, and Mount Shasta in California, are shrouded in fog, clouds, and rain and snowstorms for much of the winter months, invisible for weeks at a time. Arizona's mountains are seldom obscured for more than a few hours at a time.

We are evolved from hunters and gatherers, for whom more or less precise location at all times was vitally important. Landmarks affect us in peculiar and varied ways. Mostly they help us locate where we are, give us personal reference, and place us somewhere on a map, if only a map in our brain. Just what that map signifies varies with time, culture, and purpose. Landmarks also help define where we are and, to that extent, define us, however briefly. The permanence of landmarks contrasts with our transience. That steadfast presence also provides an anchor against excessive subjectivity, for true natural landmarks precede us and, barring cataclysmic geophysical alteration, will survive us.

Sudden (and often traumatic) alterations do occur, of course. Mount St. Helens was altered by the 1980 eruption, and though still a recognizable mountain decades later, it is transformed into a different shape. The celebrated Great Stone Face of New Hampshire collapsed in 2003. Where it once gazed down from above is now a nondescript cliff. Its disappearance was a blow to local legendry and identity. And tourism. Sunset Crater issued from more or less flat ground and in a few weeks or less changed the landscape for thousands of years to come. The upper 3,000 feet of the San Francisco Peaks appears to have slid away in one or more episodes of mass wasting. Helmet Peak appears to be doomed to be chewed up or away by the mining industry. Experts warn that Mount Rainier in Washington could be radically transformed at any time, with devastating results for Washingtonians.

Landmarks and Identity

Peoples indigenous to the Americas (or at least those having a claim to original occupation) have a long-standing tradition of holding certain places sacred, often to be approached only under controlled conditions and at certain times, and perhaps with an appropriate frame of mind. Other places, while not clearly sacred, are historically important and culturally significant. Native Americans also weave tales about the creation or origin of landmarks, attribute myths and legends to them, and endow them with personalities. We of European extraction usually find such reverence for natural places to be quaint, but for the most part hardly to be taken seriously. We apply names, but steer away from mythologies. Privatization seems an unchallengeable value for us. While most of us would prefer our most notable natural landmarks remain public, many would argue that they should be subdued and exploited to the (current) owner's benefit—and as soon as possible. Twin Peaks, a limestone landmark formerly located northwest of Tucson, has vanished, roasted in its entirety in colossal kilns into cement and transferred to human-built structures in the region and elsewhere—as concrete.

Many Native Americans consider our Eurocentric attitude seriously mistaken. They find our condescending attitude or antipathy toward reverence for landmarks a symbol of our lack of roots. Perhaps this indifference is a consequence of our ceaseless mobility, which, we must admit, is driven more by reasons of personal comfort or economic standing than by relationship to the nature of the places we choose to call home. We do find peculiar or even irrational the prohibitions issued by Native Americans restricting access to certain places. We usually view all places as up for grabs for constructing resorts or playgrounds or climbing, or places where we can surround ourselves with beauty and majesty while indulging in hedonistic pastimes. We may even resent the inconvenience we experience when we discover we may not climb Navajo Mountain, scale the summit of Shiprock, or build dams in the Grand Canyon. We view as odd the Zunis' rule that only males may approach a sacred spring and consider perplexing (though, perhaps, fortuitous) that several indigenous peoples have proposed a ban on uranium mining on New Mexico's Mount Taylor, which they consider sacred; they view mining there as sacrilegious. Some indigenous folk wonder why outsiders feel the urgency to climb to mountaintops as a matter of principle.

Anthropologist Keith Basso in his *Wisdom Sits in Places* tells us of the complex relationships between Western Apaches and places— bewilderingly complicated for us. Their culture defines places and the places define their culture. These paradigmatic places are often quite the reverse of landmarks, for they may be something as nondescript (for non-Apaches) as a meadow or a swale. But places—where historical or mythological events may have taken place—deeply affect Western Apaches' lives. They carry many levels of meaning—in placenames, in historical associations, and in the specific moral messages Apaches may wish to communicate to any of their number who might be connected with that place. All this, Basso reveals, takes place in a spiritual/physical/cultural interaction well beyond our normal European-based ability to comprehend.¶ Places take on a moral character for Western Apaches in addition to their physical descriptions.

It is common for people with long-term tenure in their homeland to observe as sacred or important not only prominences, but also places such as valleys, swales, and springs, along with individual

¶ Keith Basso, *Wisdom Sits in Places* (Albuquerque: University of New Mexico Press, 1991).

rocks, trees, bushes, and rivers, streams, or arroyos. Landmarks often inspire patriotic emotions and evoke what might seem to be ancestral memories. For example, Mexican anthropologist Diana Luque has documented 176 places on Tiburón Island in the Gulf of California (area about 450 sq. mi.) that are considered important by Seris, indigenous people who have resided in their coastal desert homelands for millennia.** The catchall term *important* covers a wide range of cultural, historical, and spiritual nuances for the Seris. Yaqui homelands in Sonora, Mexico, are laden with small to large prominences of deep cultural and spiritual importance to the Yaquis.

The same attention to place (though not to the same degree) can be found among most, if not all, indigenous groups who have occupied their territories for many centuries. Comanches have been residents of southern Texas for only a few centuries. On their arrival they found the vast, featureless plains, covered by seemingly endless scrubby forests, to be devoid of geological markers. Instead of prominences, they came to recognize certain trees as important, and even shaped them as they grew, to help mark places, pathways, and orientation. Native Floridians in the Everglades, in what appears to outsiders to be an aquatic habitat lacking readily identifiable markers, substituted waterways and forests for geological structures. The notion of harmonic convergence has its roots in ancient reckonings of place, not in New Age babble.

I spent much of the 1990s living in a village of the Mayo people of southern Sonora, Mexico. While their culture has been decimated by several centuries of military and social aggression from greater Spanish and Mexican society, pockets of solid tradition remained at that time. One of the most striking examples of stubborn cultural conservativism was a large rock located in the village of Teachive.

** Diana Luque, *Naturalezas, Saberes, y Territorios Comcáac* (Seri) (Mexico City: Instituto Nacional de Ecología, 2006).

It lies not far from the banks of Arroyo Masiaca, a major watercourse in the region, which at that time usually had a flow of water and had flowed since time immemorial. (Since the onset of the great southwestern drought beginning in the mid-1990s, the streambed has been mostly dry.) The boulder is a pleasantly rounded, water-polished massive hunk of granitic rock, somewhat over a meter in general diameter. It must have been loosed and swept from its bedrock moorings in a cataclysmic flood or earthquake from somewhere below the high granitic summit of the 1,600-meter-high Sierra de Álamos, some thirty kilometers to the north. Then it must have spent a few thousand years creeping downslope after being upended from its lodgings, broken repeatedly, and tumbled and pummeled downstream to where it came to rest in Mayo country. The rock is a solitary piece, sitting alone rather like a glacial erratic, large enough that children can clamber over it. They do.

The great rock is known in the vicinity simply as the Santa Cruz, the Holy Cross. Incised into the face of the boulder are several artistic decorations easily interpreted as crosses, messages from ancient predecessors. But the great rock is not simply left exposed on the riverbank. Villagers, one family in particular, maintain a ramada whose shade covers the Santa Cruz most of the day. At the time I frequented the area, the ramada was carefully maintained, and often decorated with bright ribbons. Candles would appear around the rock's base from time to time.

I asked several Mayos about its origins. No one was certain, but all agreed that it had been part of an earlier village of Teachive, which had been located a couple of kilometers upstream along the arroyo, at a place where water in the olden days was more plentiful. When floods destroyed the older village, perhaps some sixty or seventy years earlier, the stone monument remained as evidence of the location of now lost hamlet. Teachive was relocated to the south in a site less prone to flooding. Villagers marshalled forces to transport the Santa Cruz to its present location, which must have involved prodigious work.

I was surprised to discover, after a year or so of more or less constant presence in the village, that everyone in the area was aware of the Santa Cruz and its importance. But I discovered its presence only due to an offhand remark from a native friend of mine.

The Santa Cruz is hardly a landmark, since it was easy for me to have passed by it a dozen times without noticing it or asking about its significance. Yet it was of such importance to the nine hundred or so inhabitants of Teachive that even small children could talk about it and show me, with obvious pride, the artistic engravings—once I had learned of its existence, that is. I came to conclude that the Santa Cruz was so basic to the life of Teachive and its ancient forerunners that villagers took it for granted as an integral part of their daily life.

Elsewhere, landmarks may be markers of places of infamy or areas to be avoided, as certain peoples considered Mount Diablo near San Francisco. The first glimpse of the Sierra Nevada chilled the hearts of countless emigrants from the east hoping to settle in the Central Valley of California, knowing they had to cross the range to arrive at their goal. In contrast, native Shoshones viewed the range with awe, respect, and affection. Utes identified mountain ranges by analogies to human figures.

And there were practicalities. Engineers and planners in Chaco Canyon, New Mexico, in the eleventh century recognized that the majestic monolith that archaeologists formerly called Threatening Rock, was separating from the cliff behind the structure and was tilting toward the apartment house–style pueblo. They recognized that it would one day collapse and destroy parts of the great apartment complex we call Pueblo Bonito. But their fondness for the location—which must have entailed far more than obvious advantages—overrode their disquietudes. The rock is mostly Cliff House Sandstone, a sturdy, resistant formation of late Cretaceous age, but the underlying rock at its base—the Menefee Formation—is more easily eroded, a feature of the landscape that the architects and engineers must have noted. Chacoans worked feverishly and successfully to shore up the base of the landmark, which weighed 30,000 tons. Perhaps as a result of their preventive efforts, the rock—more than one hundred feet tall—stood for another nine hundred years. It did not fall until 1941. That rock must have been of great, and probably ominous, significance to Chacoans.

Other landmarks are of neutral emotional significance to some, serving only as markers, places such as Scotts Bluff in Nebraska or Pikes Peak in Colorado that served travelers heading west in the nineteenth century. The same Pikes Peak was emotionally charged for the Ute people of the region, who identified themselves with that peak. And the aspect and psychological significance of landmarks can change; residents of the Caribbean island of Montserrat probably altered their opinions about Soufriére Hills after it blew apart in 1995 in a volcanic explosion and destroyed most human habitations in the area. The mountain that marked their home became their enemy. Devils Tower in Wyoming was long a monument and a climbing challenge for visitors from the eastern United States. Attempts by Lakota people to prohibit climbing on that most visible of landmarks, one they considered sacred, have failed. Politically conservative outsiders sued to overturn the U.S. government's attempt to limit climbing during the month of June, a holy time for the Lakota, on the grounds that a ban would favor one religion over others, in violation of the U.S. Constitution.

For most of us, our historic mobility limits our deep attachment to landmarks of our homelands. According to a 2008 Pew Research study of the United States, hardly any of us live as adults in the homes in which we were born, and very few live in the same neighborhood. Only slightly more than a third of us live in the same town or city where we were born. Barely 40 percent of U.S. Americans live in the part of the state where they were born, and that number drops to less than one-third in the western states. During the last decade, Americans have become less inclined to move, probably a reflection of economic realities, but perhaps a trend that may strengthen our recognition of landmarks and places as important in our lives.[††] Certainly prehistoric dwellers in the Southwest were mobile as well. They moved as crop failures, overhunting, drought, or warfare forced or enticed them to move. But they moved on foot, seldom more than a few miles each day, carrying with them mental maps of the lands they left behind, to which they might well one day return. That geographical knowledge was bracketed by landmarks that identified their movements from one location to another.

Landmarks have names. Humans take comfort and pride in naming places, an act that personalizes, memorializes, and often asserts dominion. In the United States, settlers or men of power named landmarks after someone famous, often an explorer, politician, or war figure. Only rarely did women receive the honor of place-names of monuments. Spanish settlers named them after saints. Mount Whitney in the Sierra Nevada is named for a California state engineer, one who disparaged John Muir's theories of the role of glaciers in shaping the Sierras, calling him an "ignoramus." Muir, whose theories have proven correct, is honored by a trail and a redwood grove. Whitney gets his name on the highest peak in the contiguous United States. Official naming is an act of imperialism, conquest, and status. The official reversion of Mount McKinley in Alaska, the highest peak in North America, to its Athabaskan name Denali did not occur without a protest from the pro-McKinley partisans. As of 2017 loud pronouncements from the highest U.S. administrative levels proclaimed the imminent renaming of the peak after the U.S. president whose skin was white but whose meager accomplishments few can enumerate.

[††] Craig Childs in his book *The House of Rain* has noted that during the later period of Anasazi (Ancestral Pueblo) prominence in the Southwest, mobility became a necessity as a response to increasing drought and the constant threat of violence, which was primarily brought on by the drought and the attendant competition for resources. Childs, *The House of Rain* (New York: Little, Brown, 2006).

For natives, a descriptive name is more common. In the Southwest, most landmarks have but one name in each language, English or Spanish. This is not the case, as I have discovered in fieldwork in southern Mexico, where people of long tenure but with a common language may refer to a mountain by a different name in each town, especially where communities are separated by a natural barrier such as a hill or a canyon. Residents there grow up with a specific reference or viewpoint of the landmark, and its name usually reflects their position. Valleys are often separated by massive ridges, cliffs, and summits. People in another valley or on the other side of the landmark may have a different name for the same range or hill, a reflection of their isolation and familiarity with their particular view. That makes map labeling a challenge. Mapmakers try to be harmless drudges who shy away from insulting epithets.

Landmarks may have multiple personalities; or, should we say, their status may vary widely depending on the angle from which they are seen. Harry Winters, in his work on O'odham place-names, points out that indigenous naming often reflects a particular, local perspective.‡‡ A prime example of this is the dramatically different appearance between the Santa Catalina Mountains when viewed nearby from the south and when viewed nearby from the northwest. They appear to be two entirely different ranges, two distinct landmark entities, with perhaps entirely different meanings. As Winters says, some names make no sense unless the landmark is viewed from where the original namers saw it. The O'odham name for the Catalinas translates as Frog Mountain, an apt description of the mass when viewed from lands where most of the O'odham lived.

With a couple of exceptions, the landmarks selected in this book are visible from afar. More specifically, they are mostly visible from

---

‡‡ Harry Winters, *O'odham Place Names: Meanings, Origins, and Histories, Arizona and Sonora*, 2nd ed. (Tucson, Ariz.: SRI Press, 2020).

major highways in Arizona. In some ways, I find this regrettable, since motor vehicles can desecrate the very monuments they render accessible. The landmarks herein represent but a fraction of landmarks important to a society, community, or group in the Southwest. There are dozens, probably hundreds, more that have special significance to some people. It is my hope that the reader will add to this list.

A note on sources for the information in this book. Much of it, including the semi-arbitrary selection of landmarks, is based on my history and travels in the region over the last sixty years or so. I have gleaned substantial amounts of information from Web sources, too many to cite. I gathered natural history information from a wide variety of sources. More technical geological information is from far-flung sources, but include *Geology of Arizona* (Dale Nations and Edmund Stump), *Geology of the American Southwest* (Scott Baldridge), *Roadside Geology of Arizona* (Halka Chronic), *Geology Underfoot in Northern Arizona* (Lon Abbott and Teri Cook), and a marvelous but out-of-print source with superb aerial photographs, *Geology Illustrated* by John Shelton. John V. Bezy has authored several most useful and well-written descriptive books about selected sites in Arizona. Get them. Additional sources include *Landscapes of Arizona* (Terah Smiley, Dale Nations, Troy Péwé, and John Schafer), and, fundamental to lay understanding of contemporary geology, John McPhee's *Annals of the Former World*, a volume seldom far from my reach.

Agathla, north of Kayenta, near Monument Valley. Photo Dan Duncan/David Yetman.

Agathla

NORTHEASTERN ARIZONA

Brooding, dark shapes rise abruptly from the ground just north and east of Kayenta, in northeastern Arizona. They form bleak, broken ridges and peaks entirely different from the colorful cliffs and gracefully eroded formations of the adjacent landscapes.

The tallest of these sudden shapes is Agathla, which rises from the yellows and reds of Monument Valley to dominate the landscape. Agathla is a diatreme, or volcanic plug, the innards of a volcano that erupted about 25 MYA. It juts up, looming odd and mysterious. Navajos consider it sacred and powerful, as it springs nearly straight from the ground as if shot from deep within the earth. The name apparently means "some wool" in the Navajo language. The peak would have been a familiar landmark, visible to the northeast a thousand years ago to the residents of Betatakin and Keet Seel, now archaeological sites of the Kayenta Anasazi (Ancestral Pueblo) people. Its drab, forbidding volcanic color makes it appear out of place. Indeed, I find it gives off an air of warning to adventurers, a touch of Mount Doom, in dramatic contrast to the seductive, resplendent, beckoning colors of the adjacent valleys and Monument Valley. When viewed along with Chaistla Butte to the south and other volcanic outbreaks of similar age and origin, the landscape takes on an aspect out of science fiction.

Agathla's volcanic darkness is somewhat soothed, however, by muted grayish colors and gentle slopes and mounds of the Chinle Formation that flare out at its base. Also prominent in the Painted Desert far to the south, the Chinle consists of ancient mudstones from the Triassic period around 220 MYA. All are a part of Agathla's brown-gray landscape. Scaling the rock is extremely dangerous. Written permission from Navajo officials to climb the peak is mandatory, and it may be off-limits to climbers.

Agathla is the remnant of but one of several spectacular diatremes near Kayenta. Many additional volcanoes dot the Navajo volcanic field, which includes Shiprock, well to the east in New Mexico and a couple of million years older. Agathla rises more than 1,200 feet above the surrounding terrain, to an altitude of about 7,100 feet (2,164 m). For the volcano to erupt, magma—molten rock from the earth's mantle—had to force its way through the many layers of sedimentary rocks of the Colorado Plateau, the great land mass that covers the northeastern third of Arizona and much of southeastern Utah, northwestern New Mexico, and southwestern Colorado. Most of the plateau consists of blankets, thousands of feet thick, of sedimentary rocks—sandstones, mudstones, and occasional limestones—in uniform succession, much like a layer cake. That sequence is best observed in the Grand Canyon, but similar layers in the predictable order are readily observable throughout the plateau.

Chaistla Butte, Kayenta, immediately south of Agathla.

Agathla and the Navajo volcanic field represent an exception to the plateau layering. The thick strata—laid down mostly flat beginning more than 500 MYA—are occasionally penetrated from below by magma that has forced its way from the mantle to the surface, probing the crust above for weak points. Envision the original Agathla as the end of a pipe, where magma flowed and broke through to the surface. It may have encountered a large deposit of groundwater and produced an enormous explosion, resulting in a broad crater. Over many years, more magma passed and slowly clogged the pipe. The molten rock continued its relentless ride, now and then blocked by the plug. Occasionally explosive eruptions cast blocks of the rock from layers above the magma into the air and some of them fell back into the pipe. Additional magma, squeezing its way sideways and then upward through cracks, produced the prominent side features called dikes and Agathla's tortured shape.

The lava plug that we see is composed of breccia, broken chunks of lava that have hardened into durable rock. It has proved far more resistant to erosion than cinders or volcanic tuff, softer forms of volcanic rock that probably formed the sides of the erupting and exploding volcano. And it has also long outlived the rock—sandstones, mudstones, and shale—that covered the surrounding plateau at the time of the first breakthrough of magma. When that eruption occurred, the top was even with or slightly below the surface of the plateau—at least 1,200 feet above what we now see and from where Dan Duncan and I stood when he took the photograph. The pre-volcanic surface would have been Navajo Sandstone on top of Kayenta Formation on top of Wingate Formation, just as in the Vermilion Cliffs. Over the eons—25 million years or so—those rocks and layers have eroded away, scraped off and gouged out by wind and rain, leaving behind the tough volcanic rock.

Agathla's base of sloping Chinle Formation sits several hundred feet above us and the surrounding plain of Permian De Chelly Sandstone. The old surface on which the Chinle rested is about 650 feet (200 m) lower. All that missing material has been eroded away, the gravels and sand and dust deposited elsewhere and ferried down the San Juan River or a now-lost watercourse flowing in a different direction. The varying shades of gray and brown are caused by differing chemical composition of the lavas of different flows as they pushed upward toward our world.

Ash Peak, looking eastward on Arizona Route 70.

Ash Peak

ARIZONA ROUTE 70, SOUTHEAST ARIZONA

This modest but irresistibly noticeable landmark lies just inside the eastern boundary of Graham County, Arizona. It is not a massive peak nor especially high, only 5,585 feet (1,710 m) in elevation, yet it stands out as the first notable prominence in eastern Arizona on Arizona Route 70 after it crosses from New Mexico into Arizona. It is also visible to those with good distance vision to the north from Interstate 10 near San Simon. For many decades, residents of Duncan have done much of their shopping in Safford, forty miles to the west. Route 70 passes directly below Ash Peak; so it was familiar to all of Duncan's small population.

The peak is well mineralized, and several small silver mines are still in operation. In the late nineteenth century speculators announced the discovery of fabulous amounts of gold and silver on Ash Peak, and convinced eastern investors to, shall we say, assist with the costs of development. Mining operations did begin, but in 1901 an enormous explosion killed one of the mine owners and six workers. This seemed to put a damper on major mining investment, and the investors' funds evaporated. In spite of the calamity, the deposits yielded generous amounts of silver. Even now miners realize that gold and silver are to be had in Ash Peak, and the hunt continues, but on a small scale only.

Ash Peak beckons to climbers. I responded in 1955, reaching the tip with some friends after maneuvering through a cleft in the north face of the volcanic rim. A register is now located on the top, from which one can see Cochise Head in the Chiricahua Mountains far to the south and the White Mountains far to the north. Thirty miles to the west looms lofty Mount Graham, from whose summit, 5,000 feet higher, one can look down to the east and see Ash Peak, its nipple-like tip prominent, even from above. It is also the highest peak in this jumble of mountains called the Black Hills (one of several Arizona ranges so named). It is about 22 million years old and of volcanic origin, a northwestern outlier of the Peloncillo Range, whose southern limit lies in New Mexico near the Mexican border.

The Peloncillos are a volcanic chain marking a subduction zone associated with a plate boundary and general hell-raising in the Oligocene, between 25 and 34 MYA. Ash Peak appears to be part of a flow of rhyolite lava that was contained within a small crater, remnants of a volcanic explosion. The sides of the crater have faulted or eroded away, leaving the cliffs exposed, like a cupcake when its paper cover is pulled off. The tip may be a volcanic plug or part of a resurgent dome. The collection of volcanic mountains and lava flows of which it is a landmark forced the Gila River to flow to the northwest just west of Duncan. For eons the lava dams, supplemented by thick layers of volcanic ash, plugged the old river outlets to the west and trapped sediments that formed the Duncan Valley and its rich soils. Over the eons the river cut its way through the hundreds of feet of conglomerate rock and the lava dam, forming a cleft known as the Gila Box, a national recreation area administered by the Bureau of Land Management. Within the canyon, three side drainages join the Gila from the north, greatly enlarging the river.

Baboquivari Peak seen from the west. The peak is of great importance to the Tohono O'odham. It is scalable, but only with proper mountaineering equipment.

Baboquivari Peak

SOUTH-CENTRAL ARIZONA

At an elevation of 7,730 feet (2,356 m), this prominence is a triangular tower of granite, a mass of rock that dominates the adjoining valleys and plains. Baboquivari Peak is Arizona's most visible boundary landmark, and probably its most important monument. To the east of the summit are the Baboquivari Wilderness and the Altar Valley, a vast expanse of grassland, including Buenos Aires National Wildlife Refuge. To the west lie lands of the Tohono O'odham Nation. The monolith is visible from the far western reaches of the reservation, more than sixty miles to the west and well into Mexico. The peak is of great importance to the O'odham, so important that traditional O'odham hope to live in villages from which the peak is visible. "It's where the sun rises," many O'odham observe. And around sunset, the peak glows long after the remainder of the mountains are obscured in shadows and darkness.

At the western base of the peak, the Baboquivari District of the Tohono O'odham Nation has established a fine campground. Nearby is a cave dedicated to I'itoi, the creator god of the O'odham. The vegetation at the park includes an unusual mix of oaks and giant saguaro cacti. The majestic cliffs of the peak rise directly from the park. From there one can climb into the cool, moist Sycamore Canyon, home to many plants more characteristic of Mexico.

The origin of the name Baboquivari is amusing. Harry Winters, an expert on the Tohono O'odham language and place-names, reports that early Spaniards had difficulty spelling the O'odham name, Vav Giwulik, and transcribed it instead as Baboquivari. That must have been close to what they heard or thought they heard.

The peak is climbable from either side, but to reach the top one must resort to mountaineering equipment. I know, for I once participated in a wedding atop the peak. From the roomy summit, one can see far south into Mexico, and on very clear days (few in number in recent years) north to Arizona's White Mountains. To the west and north lie the vast expanses of Tohono O'odham tribal lands, over which Baboquivari Peak seems to preside.

The geology of the Baboquivari Mountains is a jumbled puzzle, only recently deciphered. Geologists label the rock of the peak itself, appropriately enough, Baboquivari Granite. Most estimates place the age of the granite on the peak at roughly 147 million years, making it late Jurassic. The lengthy range, often simply known as the Baboquivari Range, consists of several distinct mountains. To the north, Kitt Peak of the Quinlan Mountains and Coyote Peak of the Coyote Mountains are separate ranges, each geologically different from the other two.

Big Horn Mountains seen from the south. The rock seen here consists almost entirely of volcanics of different ages and origins.

Big Horn Mountains

INTERSTATE 10, WESTERN ARIZONA

Big Horn Peak rises more than 1,400 feet above the surrounding plains of southwestern Arizona, reaching nearly 3,500 feet (1,069 m) in elevation. It is strikingly visible to the north of Interstate 10 west of Tonopah, jutting up from a long ridge of arid desert mountains. The range was apparently named in the mid-nineteenth century for the abundance of bighorn sheep, which provided meat that was a favorite with both natives and U.S. Boundary Commission personnel. Parts of the range are included in the Big Horn Wilderness, which is administered by the Bureau of Land Management. It is an unusual unit of the National Wilderness Preservation System in that within its boundaries no infrastructure and no improved trails are to be found, even though it offers some of the Sonoran Desert's finest habitats and is rich with wildlife, a true wilderness. Visitors may find temperatures in the late spring, summer, and early fall to be excessive, perhaps life-threatening. A maximum temperature of 120 degrees is not unusual. In the summer of 2020, nearby Phoenix, usually a few degrees cooler than the Big Horns, registered fifty-five days with temperatures of 110 degrees Fahrenheit or above.

The Big Horn Range as seen from I-10 is a graphic example of the volcanism present in western Arizona around 20 MYA. Wave after wave of lava flows, ash flows, pyroclastic flows, and explosions would have treated anyone around to a colossal display. If, that is, one had a few thousand years to wait between explosive events. Downtime vastly exceeded time of volcanic activity. Beneath those thick layers of Miocene volcanism is an extremely complicated base of very old rock that has been churned and mixed over the eons.

The entire range has been known for its gold deposits, though the cover of volcanic rock makes the southern reaches of the range unattractive to prospectors. Desert mountain ranges of volcanic origin are often home to concentrated (though usually small) deposits of gold and silver. Volcanic forces tend to concentrate metallic salts when magma encounters water. The superheated water dissolves the salts, which precipitate out in pockets when the magma cools. Over millions of years rainwater, meager though it may be, filters through the soil from the surface into the underlying rock. When that water reaches those deposits, it greatly concentrates the metals through a process called supergene enrichment. Because the rains are sparse, the amount that penetrates is small and is confined to the upper levels of the rock. If more water seeped through, it would dilute and flush the metallic salts far into the lower rock.

These deposits, sometimes of nearly pure metal, are often near ground level, and seasoned prospectors readily identify them. Though they are often of only minor size—sometimes only a few feet deep—the ore of these enriched sites is concentrated enough to make hard rock mining profitable, sometimes very profitable. At least for a little while. At other times they may be huge—most of our great copper mines are located in arid or semiarid areas and feature a similar geological history. A local example is the Vulture Mine in the Vulture Mountains close to Wickenburg, Arizona, east of the Big Horn Mountains. It produced fabulous amounts of gold before closing in 1942. The Big Horns are pocked with small mines that followed promising lodes but have not struck it rich.

Bill Williams Mountain seen from near Interstate 40 at Williams. Photo by Dan Duncan.

Bill Williams Mountain

INTERSTATE 40, NORTHWESTERN ARIZONA

From the old lumber town of Williams, a large dome-shaped mountain looms to the south. At an elevation of 9,256 feet (2,821 m), Bill Williams Mountain is the highest peak in the western half of Arizona and dominates the skyline on the south side of Interstate 40 west of Flagstaff for many miles. Though its summit is rounded rather than jagged, the mountain is visible far to the south—I saw it routinely from several viewpoints in Prescott, where I lived for many years. It juts above the southwestern end of the Colorado Plateau where the Mogollon Rim ends as it pinches off toward the northwest into a series of rough and wild canyons. Several sensational trails begin on the southern slopes of the mountain and descend through the convoluted rim country into the Transition Zone and Basin and Range of central and western Arizona. Other trails, including a dirt road, lead to the summit of the mountain, which is partially swathed in dense groves of aspen and coniferous forests.

The mountain is named after a famed and eccentric mountain man—fur trapper, guide, and scout for parties of Europeans. He worked the region and was fluent in many indigenous languages. Williams was killed in a battle with Utes in 1849. A large drainage west of the mountain bears his name as well. It forms a major tributary of the lower Colorado River and marks the boundary between La Paz and Mohave Counties.

Bill Williams Mountain is an extinct volcano, or, more accurately, a series of extinct volcanoes. The volcanic activity here is the point farthest west where volcanoes of the San Francisco volcanic field—which contains remnants of six hundred volcanoes—appear on the landscape. The volcanoes of Bill Williams Mountain are the oldest, as much as 6 million years old. To the east, the volcanoes become younger and younger. The San Francisco Peaks, part of the same volcanic field as Bill Williams, are about 2 million years old. Sunset Crater, one of the farthest to the east in the field, is but a thousand years old.

The source of the magma responsible for the volcanic activity appears to be moving east. Or, more probably, it is more or less stationary deep beneath the Colorado Plateau, which sits on top of the magma chamber that is forever seeking weak spots in the earth's crust. Many geologists believe the entire plateau is ever so slowly being drawn west by extension as the Pacific Plate pulls off to the northwest, perhaps dragging the North American Plate (on which the San Francisco volcanic field sits) over a magma hotspot. The plateau's western edge lies a few miles west of Williams. There, I-40 descends abruptly, leaving the Colorado Plateau and the volcano field behind.

Boundary Cone. This volcanic plug is a landmark for those living along the Colorado River, twelve miles away.

Boundary Cone

OATMAN, MOHAVE COUNTY

Boundary Cone is a prominent landmark in extreme western Arizona on Bureau of Land Management lands, an outlier of the Black Mountains. It overlooks the Colorado River valley, Fort Mojave Indian Reservation, and Bullhead City. Its significance to native peoples has led to its inclusion in the National Register of Historic Places.

The monument is composed of volcanic rock between 18 and 19 million years old. The cone is a remainder (and reminder) of a truly massive exhalation of volcanic material—1,000 cubic kilometers of it—during the early Miocene, a period that created the Black Mountains. That range is a fine example of Basin and Range extension and at seventy-five miles in length is the longest in Arizona. The Black Mountains contain Arizona's most convoluted and dramatic volcanic landscapes, a bewildering assemblage of contorted, twisted, folded, and upchurned rock in a variety of colors. Old Route 66 west of Kingman penetrates the mountains in a lengthy slow-motion stretch, a truly stomach-churning series of turns without guard rails. Road signs constantly warn motorcyclists to be vigilant. The bars of Oatman are not too distant.

Boundary Cone is similar in construction to Agathla and Shiprock. The lavas that make up the diatreme, or plug, are resistant to weathering, more so than the original material that formed the sides of the volcano. While Boundary Cone rises a mere 750 feet above its base, it is a solitary marker and visible from afar when the view is not blocked by other formations of the Black Mountains.

Oatman is the closest town to Boundary Cone. The quaint old place is located about four miles north of the landmark, in the heart of the Black Mountains. Above it looms a startlingly white monolith of rhyolite named Elephant Tooth (see p. 24). Route 66 passes through Oatman's main and only street. The place struggles by as a somewhat glamorized ghost town, though nearby a vigorously worked open pit mine has breathed more commercial life into the old town. Oatman's mines produced gold worth more than $30 million in the late nineteenth and early twentieth centuries before closing in the 1930s. After that, its destiny lay in the hands of travelers on Route 66. With the opening of the much faster and infinitely safer Interstate 40, the town was largely abandoned. In the cooler months it becomes a rather lively place, with semi-resident feral burros stalking the streets and ample, though intermittent entertainment available, primarily oriented toward the young and restless. And thirsty. And weary of conventional consciousness. Small packets of fodder for the ubiquitous burros are available for only one dollar. Just remember that burros are a devious lot.

Camelback Mountain viewed from Papago Park in east Phoenix. Photo by Dan Duncan.

Camelback Mountain

PHOENIX

Camelback Mountain is the landmark probably seen daily by more Arizonans than any other. When Mesa, Phoenix, Scottsdale, and Tempe were founded in the late nineteenth century (keep in mind that Walpi, on the Hopi Reservation, was founded about one thousand years earlier), the mountain marked the northern end of the Phoenix metropolitan area and continued to do so through the 1950s. Since then the burgeoning cities and new tracts have moved relentlessly north and east, gradually surrounding the landmark with a seemingly endless and uniform urban landscape.

Prior to Arizona's statehood in 1912, the mountain was included within the Salt River Indian Reservation, but powerful economic interests and politicians successfully pressured the territorial legislature and the federal government to remove Camelback and a huge chunk of land from the reservation in order to make it available to non-Indians (i.e., land speculators and developers). Private development then gradually encroached on the mountain and began to creep up the sides, until the 1960s when a public campaign to save the mountain took hold and the remaining parts of the mountain were made into a public park. The area around the mountain, especially the lower slopes, continues to harbor homes and offices of many of the elite of the Salt River Valley. Camelback Road, an east-west arterial street that cuts through the southern slopes, begins just east of the mountain's limits and extends for more than thirty miles to the west to an area where the mountain is barely noticeable.

Centuries before settlers from the eastern United States found the mountain to be attractive, native peoples were expressing its importance for them. Archaeologists have discovered artifacts in caves on the north side of the mountain that establish it as a culturally significant site. The Akimeli O'odham, or River Pimas as outsiders called them, continue to view Camelback as a sacred place. It has become popular with rock climbers, as well as crowds of hikers.

The top of Camelback Mountain sits at 2,707 feet (825 m), roughly 1,300 feet above its base. It is but one peak in a small range called the Phoenix Mountains but presents an intriguing geological puzzle. The highest portions of the mountain are composed of Proterozoic granite somewhere around 1.5 billion years of age. Lower rocks of the mountain are far younger, and the reddish sandstone that forms the camel's head on the northwest side is from Tertiary-Oligocene times, 25–30 MYA. So older rock blankets rock that is far, far younger. Geologists continue to work extracting the details about the mountain's deep history. The story lies obscured in the misty saga of Arizona's geological beginnings, more than 1.7 billion years ago, when the entirety of the Salt River Valley lay beneath a sea in which volcanoes were constantly erupting. Remnants of the murky period are visible in the ancient rock of Camelback. An odd phenomenon of the mountain is the absence of rock from the Paleozoic through the Mesozoic periods, 541–66 MYA, meaning that 500 million years of geological history are absent. On the camel's head, Miocene volcanics (20 million years of age or so) sit on Precambrian rock. What went on for those missing hundreds of millions of years is not recorded in the Phoenix Mountains.

Cathedral Rock, Sedona. The upright pillars are mostly Schnebly Hill Formation, found here but absent from the Grand Canyon. Photo by Dan Duncan.

Cathedral Rock

OAK CREEK CANYON, SEDONA

Oak Creek, a tributary of the Verde River, is one of Arizona's few reliably perennial streams, though modest by most standards. Near Sedona the creek and its tributaries have carved out Oak Creek Canyon, over which Cathedral Rock presides. Its towers and ridges have been excavated by eons of erosion caused by wind, ice, and rain. The creek itself quite opportunistically follows a fault that separates one side of the canyon from the other, enlarging what tectonic forces have previously wrought.

Since the early twentieth century the Sedona landmarks have probably been second only to the Grand Canyon as natural tourist attractions in Arizona. Slide Rock, a chute through which Oak Creek rushes, has been a popular Arizona swimming hole for more than a century and is now a state park. It was a tradition at my alma mater, Prescott High School, for seniors to take off one day and spend it at Slide Rock. I hope it is still the case. Adjacent was one of Arizona's earliest apple orchards, for Sedona was one of the few places in Arizona where good apples could be raised, a fact I happily shared with my classmates, though the trees were barely in bloom. Sedona has grown from a small town when I first visited in the mid-1950s into a crowded, expensive tourist haven.

Readily viewed from Arizona Route 179, Cathedral Rock and nearby Bell Rock became popular in the later twentieth century as a supposed center of harmonic convergence. Sedona officials and business leaders smiled tolerantly and nodded appreciatively at this designation as tourists, most of them affluent, poured in to experience cosmological awakening. The viewer must decide whether Cathedral Rock is a place of mystical power or merely one of transcendent beauty.

Cathedral Rock is a most notable formation in a land of astonishing varieties of monuments. The pink-to-orange landmark is a prominent manifestation of the Schnebly Hill Formation, a grouping of sublayers that together form a distinctive band at this location on the edge of the Colorado Plateau. The formation provides the backdrop for Sedona and constitutes much of the color and texture for Oak Creek Canyon. Though Thunder Mountain to the north is taller and more imposing, Cathedral Rock is the more famous. Its penetrating color and distinct sculpturing stem from the presence of the Schnebly Hill Formation. About 270 million years old—surviving from Permian times—the formation is a mixture of layers mostly of sandstone and a thin layer of limestone, derived from a sea coastal environment formed by windblown sand dunes, on the one hand, and lake or marine deposits, on the other. These strata were laid as the sea advanced and declined from the southeast. When the sea departed, deserts encroached and receded. The reddish color throughout the formation is due to the presence of iron in the sandstone.

The Schnebly Hill Formation is widespread in the Sedona area, where it reaches a thickness of about 700 feet. It is absent from the Grand Canyon. The reason: the ancient seas—whose sands accumulated for eons and hardened into the formation—reached their northern limit in the Sedona area. And thus, the Sedona area boasts a major geologic feature not found in the Grand Canyon. Elsewhere, geological strata are shared by the two famous canyons. The gentler slopes below the Schnebly Hill Formation are a thick layer of Hermit Shale, also found in the Grand Canyon. Below the Hermit Shale is a modest layer of Supai Sandstone, which abounds throughout the western portion of the Colorado Plateau. (Some geologists refer to the entire sequence, including Schnebly Hill Formation, as the Supai Group.) And capping the Schnebly Hill Formation are the cliffs of whitish Coconino Sandstone, the heritage of millions of years of massive sand dunes in motion and a prominent feature of the Grand Canyon layering. Atop Cathedral Rock only a small cap of the Coconino remains. However, the bulk of upper Thunder Mountain, on the left side of the photo, is a prominent example of its thickness, which may exceed 500 feet. The Permian-age Coconino covers thousands of square miles of the Colorado Plateau and constitutes one of the upper layers of the canyon and cliff walls that tower over Sedona to the north. Farther away, atop the Mogollon Rim, Coconino Sandstone is in turn capped by cliffs of tough Kaibab Limestone, of late Permian age. It is the top layer of the rock of the Grand Canyon as well. These higher layers are composed of more durable material than some of the lower layers, which are more easily eroded. Above the Kaibab Limestone along portions of the rim a layer of hard basaltic lava provides an additional resistant layer.

Oak Creek Canyon itself demonstrates the power of erosion. Over time, the weaker underlying material is being worn away, causing the more resistant higher layers to become unstable and, at some point, to collapse or topple. This is the ongoing saga of the Mogollon Rim, the nearly three-hundred-mile-long array of cliffs to the north and east that form the edge of Oak Creek Canyon and the southern edge of the Colorado Plateau. The rim's edge, which looms two to nearly three thousand feet above Sedona, has retreated some four miles over the last 25 million years as the plateau concedes ground to the Transition Zone. The rim has been relentlessly undermined and thus retreated. Along the way some masses of rock remained intact because they were capped by more resistant rock—Coconino Sandstone or much younger lavas that flowed freely through the region long before the eruptions of the San Francisco volcanic field. Cathedral Rock is one such example of a surviving monument, for its cap of the Coconino Sandstone affords it some protection from erosion. However, the great rock is not composed entirely of Schnebly Hill Formation sedimentary rocks. In the middle of the Cathedral (not visible in the photograph), the visitor can spot a dark, shiny, head-like formation, more or less vertical. This is a rather young volcanic plug resulting from magma that worked its way through the layers, probably some 15 MYA. You have to be impressed by its persistence.

As you admire Cathedral Rock, be aware that behind you lies the Transition Zone Province of Arizona, where rocks that are more than one billion years older than anything around Sedona intermingle with younger volcanics in a confused jumble. The convenient layering of the Colorado Plateau is no longer available as an educational tool. The relatively flat-topped range to the west and south is Mingus Mountain, part of the Black Hills (one of several ranges in Arizona with the same name). They harbor a vastly different history and a drab exterior compared with Cathedral Rock.

Mount Tipton, Cerbat Mountains. The summit harbors pine forests. The nondescript colors belie enormous mineral deposits within the Cerbats.

Cerbat Mountains, Mount Tipton

U.S. 93, MOHAVE COUNTY

The Cerbat Mountains lie to the east of U.S. 93 that links Kingman with Hoover Dam and Las Vegas, Nevada. Kingman lies between the Cerbats to the north and the Hualapais to the south. Interstate 40 follows a pass that splits the two ranges. The Cerbat's highest point, Mount Tipton, in the northern part of the range, rises to about 7,150 feet (2,179 m), nearly 5,000 feet above the adjacent basins. This high point is largely protected within the Mount Tipton Wilderness. The Cerbat Mountains present a classic case of Basin and Range orientation. They measure about twenty-five miles in length and are oriented generally southeast to northwest. They are surrounded on all sides by the Mohave Desert. Unlike the Sonoran Desert, the Mohave (or Mojave, according to Californians) receives most of its rain during the cooler months and experiences chilly winters. As a result, the vegetation of the region is mostly different from that of southern and southwestern Arizona.

Immediately to the east of the Cerbat Mountains is the barren Hualapai Basin, which for eons has collected sediments shed from the Cerbats to the west and from the Grand Wash Cliffs, the western edge of the Colorado Plateau, to the east. To the west of Mount Tipton and the Cerbats are the very arid Sacramento Basin and the aptly named Detrital Basin, into which both the Cerbats and the Black Mountains to the west have dumped sediments for the last 15 million years or so. Those basins have proven ideal for construction of a highway that enables vice-hungry southwesterners to drive painlessly to Las Vegas. Some lose their taste for the high life shortly thereafter. Others find hardened addiction.

Most of the exposed rock of the northern portion of the Cerbats is ancient—around 1.7 billion years old. Near the semi-ghost town of Chloride, around the center of the range, a volcanic eruption occurred some 70 MYA. The magma from that activity produced superheated water that dissolved numerous metal-bearing rocks, which then precipitated out as the liquids cooled, producing pockets and veins of ore. And so, the Chloride area has been the scene of a hodgepodge of mines, beginning in the 1880s. Copper deposits in the nearby Mineral Park mine of the Cerbats are among the largest known in the world. The ore body is renowned for its turquoise as well. Chloride is now home to a few hundred hardy retirees. Mine tailings still dominate the town's landscape.

The ridgeline of the Chiricahua Mountains viewed from near Apache Pass, Sulphur Springs Valley, on the west side of the range. Chiricahua Peak at 9,755 feet elevation is in the center.

Chiricahua Mountains

EASTERN COCHISE COUNTY

The Chiricahua Mountains are unmistakably prominent south of Interstate 10 between Bowie and the New Mexico state line. (See also Cochise Head, next entry, and entry for Portal Peak and Silver Peak.) They are the best known of the sky islands of southern Arizona and New Mexico. Sky islands are peaks and ranges surrounded by desert with multiple habitats between their bases and their summits. The Chiricahuas extend more than forty miles north to south and are about twenty miles wide. The highest peak is Chiricahua Peak at an elevation of 9,755 feet (2,973 m). The range is thus high enough and large enough to contain a remarkable variety of habitats, a convergence of biomes with influences from the north, east, and south, resulting in biological diversity unmatched elsewhere. The higher ridges have a substantial area above 8,000 feet, which has given rise to an extensive mixed conifer forest, now much depleted by a fire that decimated the range in 2011. Those forests had been lumbered extensively from the late nineteenth century until the 1950s. The canyons of the Chiricahuas' west side widen toward their mouths, merging into gentle slopes populated by most agreeable forests of great oaks interspersed with lush grasslands. These were home to Apaches in the eighteenth and nineteenth centuries, perhaps centuries earlier. They found there a rich source of edible plant materials and wild game capable of supporting a substantial population. The vast grasslands to the west, depicted in the photograph, are home to large ranches where cattle still feast on the abundant forage. The east side of the range is lower and considerably drier, for the Chiricahuas create a rain shadow that deprives lands to the east of moisture milked from cyclonic storms by the higher slopes. Most of the range visible from the western side is a result of a cataclysmic volcanic explosion in late Oligocene times—about 26.5 MYA—that left behind the Turkey Creek caldera, the eastern edge of which is partially visible in the photo. Geologists working in the late 1960s with the late Paul Damon, a giant in the field and a friend of mine, discovered the caldera using satellite photos. The blast or blasts—part of the general volcanic activity in the region during the late Oligocene—spewed out colossal amounts of rhyolite, sufficient to smother much of the range and beyond with a deep blanket of volcanic rock. Perhaps 10 million years later Basin and Range faulting raised the mountains to their present height. (See further descriptions in the Cochise Head entry, below.) The drainages of the west side find their way into the Willcox Playa, a closed basin that during Pleistocene times was a substantial lake. It is a dry and dusty wasteland for much of the year, but often retains pockets of surface waters with sufficient biological productivity to make them temporary home to flocks of sandhill cranes.

I lived with my family in a canyon on the west side of the range for nearly four years and managed to hike most of that slope's myriad trails, a product of the Civilian Conservation Corps during the Great Depression. Bear sign were everywhere at that time. I believe that is still the case, but nowadays many of those trails can no longer be discerned.

Cochise Head looking north from Massai Point, Chiricahua National Monument.

Cochise Head and Chiricahua National Monument

SOUTHEASTERN ARIZONA

Cochise Head's likeness to the head of a man wearing a headdress looks remarkably the same whether viewed from Interstate 10 near San Simon on the north or from the Massai Point parking lot in Chiricahua National Monument on the south. In the eighteenth and nineteenth centuries (perhaps much earlier) the Chiricahua Mountains were part of the land of the Chiricahua Apache and commemorating their presence and that of their great leader is appropriate. Farther south lies the crest of the Chiricahuas, which reaches nearly 10,000 feet in elevation. A single road crosses the crest, connecting Rodeo, New Mexico, with Willcox, Arizona. A foot trail along the crest leads into the Chiricahua Wilderness. It was assaulted in 2011 by a crown forest fire that lasted for weeks. Much of the relict coniferous forest was burned and as of 2020 showed little signs of recovery. Other parts of the Chiricahuas have shown robust recovery.

From the summit of Cochise Head at 8,113 feet (2,473 m), the high Chiricahuas look like a distant range to the south, while farther east the long swing of the Peloncillo Mountains appears as an irregular furrow in the earth's crust, swinging from the north, to the east, and far to the southeast.

The rock of Cochise Head is rhyolite, virtually the same as that found eroded into innumerable hoodoos within the monument. The thick deposit of rhyolite stems from spectacular volcanic explosions some 26.5 MYA that shaped the crest of the Chiricahuas into much the same form we see now. Today's range, however, has been significantly eroded and parts of it hidden beneath sediments as it tilted westward through Basin and Range extension and faulting. The crest represents the rim of the crater after things settled out.

Cochise Head seen from the north along Interstate 10 near San Simon.

Chiricahua National Monument's numerous hoodoos are its principal attraction, but its canyons also offer some unusual scenery and biological features. Rock rattlesnakes (*Crotalus lepidus*), a protected species, are surprisingly abundant, and in the moist canyon bottoms large Arizona cypresses (*Cupressus arizonica*) seem to thrive. In years when rain is abundant, the canyons, seldom visited, offer inviting pools to those willing to hop over some rough boulders.

Dos Cabezas seen from the west near Willcox. Government Peak is barely visible on the extreme right above the closer ridge.

Dos Cabezas

INTERSTATE 10, COCHISE COUNTY

Dos Cabezas means "two heads" in Spanish, and the basis for the name is evident from Interstate 10 between Bowie and Willcox. The heads were a landmark on the early overland route between the Rio Grande in New Mexico and the San Pedro and Santa Cruz Rivers in Arizona and later Tucson. On a clear day they are still visible from fifty miles to the east, less from the west where taller mountains and air pollution block the view. The higher of the two heads sits at 8,254 feet (2,516 m). Apache Pass on the southeast side of the range follows the divide (based on a major fault) between the Dos Cabezas Mountains and the northern foothills of the Chiricahua Mountains. Fort Bowie National Historic Site lies immediately east of the pass. The semi-ghost town of Dos Cabezas is set on the western side.

At the eastern end of the range and towering above the pass is Government Peak, named by military personnel asserting their dominion over the region. From there, following the Civil War, scouts, whether employed by the U.S. government or loyal to Apaches, could readily observe any traffic over Apache Pass. I will certify that it is possible to climb to the base of the two heads from the ghost town of Dos Cabezas and then follow the ridgeline east, summiting on Government Peak, and finally dropping down to the roadway (dirt) connecting I-10 with Fort Bowie and Chiricahua National Monument.

The Dos Cabezas Range formed independently from the Chiricahua Mountains to the east and is heavily mineralized. The mountain is pockmarked with mines, some of which are still worked. The mines explain the existence of the town, which has been there since the 1870s (by then the defiant Apaches had been "pacified") and once was large enough to house a post office.

The Apache Pass Fault, which technically separates the two ranges, is a strike-slip fault, one in which the two sides of the fault move by each other horizontally, as does the San Andreas Fault. The Apache Pass Fault is offset—that is, points formerly side by side on the two sides have been separated by plate motion—by nearly eight miles. Water from the Chiricahua side of the fault seeps through the porous rock on the Chiricahua side and encounters the impermeable, alien rock on the west side and, with nowhere else to go, finds its way to the surface. There, it emerges as a spring, the faithful spring that provided water for Fort Bowie. Its flow proved sufficient to supply the fort and its soldiery, whose job was to fend off attacks from Apaches and, ultimately, make southern Arizona safe for settlers from the East, who found Apache lands much to their liking.

The Dos Cabezas Range is home to exposed Pinal Schist, the oldest rock in southern Arizona and considered its "basement," nearly 1.7 billion years old, and with a thickness of nearly 20,000 feet (6,000 m). Other rock of early Precambrian age also abounds. The mountains have been shot through with much younger (though still ancient) volcanic activity when magma managed to squeeze through the ancient schist. The enormous heat from that molten mass produced steam, which dissolved large quantities of metallic compounds and deposited them later as the rock cooled, producing ore bodies that were then concentrated by contact with surface waters.

The two heads are formed of welded tuff and, apparently, rhyolite, volcanic rocks deposited on top of the existing rock, probably near the end of the Cretaceous period, about 66 MYA, nearly 40 million years before the explosion in the Chiricahuas that created the Turkey Creek caldera. The volcanic portion of the mountains was far higher after the volcanic period at the end of the Cretaceous. Millions of years of erosion cleared away the upper layers, leaving behind the "heads," which appear to be plugs from a volcanic vent.

Dragoon Mountains, northwest side, seen from near Interstate 10.

Dragoon Mountains

INTERSTATE 10, COCHISE COUNTY

The Dragoon Mountains are not especially prominent from a distance, reaching only slightly over 7,500 feet (2,286 m) in elevation. They are not a large range, either, barely twenty-five miles in length and ten in width. They are not known for streams, diverse habitat, or forests. No single peak stands out. Their importance in Arizona history can hardly be exaggerated, however, due to their unmatched complexity, especially the abundance of massive granite formations and outcrops. This display makes the range visually distinct and a laboratory illustrating the peculiar tendency for granite to form massive boulders. The proliferation of granite, weathered into innumerable but invariably rounded shapes, has produced a landscape with myriad potential hideouts, hidden streams, intimate valleys, and observation points. And it makes for most agreeable hiking.

The range is named for the U.S. cavalry dragoons who encamped in the range in 1856, only three years after the signing of the Gadsden Purchase brought the mountains into the United States. U.S. troops began to frequent the area to claim it from Apaches, who had been using it as their home for at least two hundred years, perhaps far more, and had resisted settlers. While they launched occasional attacks on military targets and settlers from the United States, Apaches for the most part allowed Americans to pass through their territory and even allowed some to settle therein. They preferred to conduct their raids into Mexico, returning to Arizona Territory with their booty. In 1861, after a military blunder by U.S. Cavalry that resulted in the massacre of Apaches, their leader Cochise took up their banner of resistance. He began to conduct guerrilla activities against American settlers and troops, basing his operation mostly in the Dragoon Mountains, where small numbers of Apaches could hold off much larger numbers of American troops. His legendary abilities as a leader produced despair among settlers, ranchers, farmers, and miners, who had been encouraged by the U.S. government to settle in Apache territory in the newly acquired region. In 1872 Cochise agreed to a truce, which held until after his death in 1874. He is supposedly buried somewhere in the Dragoons.

Cochise Stronghold bears his name, even though it was never a major camp or hangout for Apaches. As visitors can see, it is a most desirable place to camp, but would be vulnerable to attack far more than Apaches would fancy. They held up in less vulnerable locations in the range.

The Dragoons are now host to a network of trails that lead well into the intricate granite labyrinths and the higher slopes, which give the visitor an idea of the usefulness of the range to Apaches.

Mid-Tertiary Stronghold Granite, Dragoon Mountains.

The range is a mixture of Precambrian, Paleozoic, and Mesozoic rock, but the dominant feature by far is Stronghold Granite, which gives the range its rugged character. While the age of the granite is still debated, it appears to be somewhere between 20 and 25 million years of age, that is, mid-Tertiary or Miocene (or perhaps late Oligocene), the time when a large pluton of magma intruded into the ancient rock above. Subsequent erosion and Basin and Range tilting have brought the granite to the surface, to our great advantage. The granite's peculiar tendency to weather along joints and form rounded boulders is especially evident in the Dragoons. The phenomenon is also evident in Texas Canyon in the north, which is located in the Little Dragoon Mountains just to the north. These have different geological origins, and the exposed granites there are far older.

Escudilla Mountain, seen from U.S. 180 near Nutrioso, shows the effects of a 2011 forest fire that swept the mountain.

Escudilla Mountain

EASTERN ARIZONA

Escudilla Mountain is quite large, but its lack of relief belies its size. A forest fire burned the entire mountain in 2011, and in this photo, taken seven years later, the once-dense forest shows little sign of recovery.

The name means simply "bowl" in Spanish, apparently referring to a possible interpretation of its shape when inverted. Even though this huge mass of lava rises around 2,400 feet above its base in the eastern White Mountains, it is one of Arizona's lesser known monuments, probably because it lacks sharply defined peaks, ridges, and rock outcroppings. At an elevation of about 10,900 feet (3,222 m), it is also Arizona's third highest peak, that is, if we view the San Francisco Peaks and Mount Baldy each as one large summit, rather than consider the individual high points in the vicinity. On clear days, rare in our times, the mountain is visible from more than fifty miles away.

Escudilla Mountain is best viewed from Nutrioso, appearing from this village as an imposing lump to the east. It has experienced double misfortune in the last seventy years, having been torched by firestorms in 1951 and again in 2011. I first saw the mountain in 1954, and scars from the earlier fire were still evident, for most of the timber had been consumed by the fire, brought about by a long history of forest mismanagement and the drought of the 1950s. Reforestation was remarkable through the end of the twentieth century, and fir, spruce, pine, and aspen returned in abundance, but the drought of the late twentieth and early twenty-first centuries created another tinderbox. The Bear Wallow Fire began in the White Mountains on May 11, 2011, and continued to burn through early July. The burn consumed more than 500,000 acres, much of it in heavy Ponderosa pine timber, but including other habitats as well. It ultimately spread into western New Mexico. It was the largest fire in recorded Arizona history. As of 2019, the burned Escudilla Mountain showed few signs of recovery of the forest, largely because of the ongoing drought and the heat generated by the Bear Wallow Fire that was so intense it destroyed seeds.

The mountain now remains largely colorless, as the photograph demonstrates. If rains return, we can hope to see bright green groves of quaking aspen and, over the decades, reforestation by pines and perhaps firs. Whether the splendid stands of Engelmann spruce return will depend on the return of both summer and winter rains. Long-range forecasts predict hotter and drier conditions throughout the Southwest, which bodes ominous for return of the mountain's thick forests.

Most geologists consider Escudilla to be part of the Mogollon-Datil volcanic field that extends eastward to the Rio Grande Rift in New Mexico and includes the Gila Mountains of New Mexico. The mountain is a remnant of a large volcano that stands out in an area replete with volcanic activity that has continued up to the last 300,000 years. The rock at the summit of Escudilla is of late Oligocene age, 26–24 MYA, more than 15 million years older than the volcanics of Mount Baldy, only twenty miles to the west. Baldy is a shield volcano, that is, a volcano built up from multiple layers of lava, dating from about 9 MYA. It is more than 11,000 feet in elevation, but its summit is the culmination of a gradual uplift and not a standout landmark.

Escudilla's volcanic rock is also around 20 million years older than the volcanic outpourings of the Springerville volcanic field, fifteen miles to the north. Large exposures of sandstone on the southern side of Escudilla Mountain are also proof that its origin is decidedly different from the volcanic masses of the Springerville volcanic field, whose basalts date from 300,000–6 million years of age. In the case of Escudilla, andesite lavas, often more explosive than basalts, flowed over the sandstone and built up to an elevation considerably greater than what we now see. It has been pared down by erosion. The Springerville volcanic field is home to more than four hundred cinder cones and volcanic vents, which popped and fumed for a few million years, erupting from the earth but never achieving great size. Meanwhile, Escudilla Mountain, long extinct, brooded far above in stony silence, powerless to prevent its size from being whittled down by naturally destructive forces.

Four Peaks, Mazatzal Mountains, seen from Usery Mountain Regional Park, Mesa, Arizona. The rock of the peaks is far older than the rock on which it sits.

Four Peaks, Mazatzal Range

EASTERN MARICOPA COUNTY

Four Peaks, a rugged series of nearly equal summits, towers over the southern portion of the wild and varied Mazatzal Range. (Local folk often pronounce the name, incorrectly, MAA-tah-zal, a strange twist.) Most of the range lies to the east of the Verde River, which runs north to south in central Arizona and flows into the Salt River near Phoenix. Fine views of the peaks can be had from Arizona Route 87, the Beeline Highway that connects the Salt River Valley and Payson.

The Mazatzals are largely roadless wilderness, perhaps the roughest in Arizona, a vast, jumbled, mountainous expanse of grabbing and whipping chaparral and unforgiving boulders. The Verde River forms much of the western boundary of the southern half of the Mazatzal Wilderness, a tract of just over 250,000 acres that is part of Tonto National Forest. Four Peaks lies within the wilderness (since it is one unit, I refer to it in the singular) and is the most prominent mountain visible from Phoenix, especially from the eastern portions of the Salt River Valley. In winter, it is often snow-capped, a handsome aesthetic enhancement to the Phoenix area, where snow is virtually unknown. Four Peaks is also visible from Tonto National Monument to the east, where the pre-Columbian Salado culture inhabitants must have enjoyed views of the snow. In 2020 a wildfire consumed an enormous tract of the Mazatzal Wilderness, leaving behind a scorched wasteland that will take decades or centuries to recover.

The highest peak in the Mazatzals, called Brown's Peak, is 7,659 feet (2,334 m) in elevation, the highest point in Maricopa County. The hike to the summits is notorious for its difficulty, for trails are rudimentary. Four Peaks is home to an amethyst mine producing some of the world's finest stones. The highest quality products are gems of an alluring shade of purple.

The rock from which the peaks are formed is very old, consisting of Precambrian Mazatzal quartzite, an unusually durable metamorphic rock, one of the hardest in the Southwest. Quartzite is quartz sand that has been metamorphosed, that is, subjected to extreme heat and pressure. Its hardness explains why the peaks have endured for nearly 1.7 billion years while all other competing rocks have eroded away. Ironically, younger granite rocks lie farther down the slopes below and beneath the quartzite. At one point about a hundred million years after the emplacement of the quartzite, it was intruded by magma from a pluton that nearly reached the surface and forced the peaks upward as though they were floating on rising dough. Over a few million years the magma cooled to form granite, which appears at the base of the peaks. It was as if a room in a house filled with foam under pressure so that the roof was raised and moved, engulfed in foam. The intrusion of the magma resulted, some geologists claim, in a geological phenomenon known as a roof pendant, an area where the magma contacted existing ceiling rock and completely engulfed it and changed its character (contact metamorphism). Over hundreds of millions of years, the granite (and other rock, from epoch to epoch, less resistant than the quartzite), has eroded away from the top, leaving the tough quartzite increasingly exposed. Much of that granite remains lower on the mountains throughout the Mazatzal Range. It has weathered into vast fields of rounded, agreeable, though intimidating boulders.

The peaks and the granite on which they rest have been uplifted several times, the last rise probably during the late Laramide orogeny, somewhere around 50 MYA. Unless a cataclysmic volcanic eruption covers the peaks with ash and tuff, they will remain much unchanged millions of years after the ruins of Phoenix have been reduced to indecipherable dust. Except, maybe, for plastic bags.

Inside Granite Dells, U.S. 89, Central Arizona. Elevation 5,100 feet.

Granite Dells

U.S. 89, PRESCOTT

The mountainous terrain around the city of Prescott is dominated by outcroppings of granite in the form of pleasantly rounded, often house-sized boulders and hillsides of seemingly endless rounded and creviced rock. In this hodgepodge of boulders, hills, and mountains, Granite Dells, located along U.S. 89 a few miles north of the city, is especially noticeable. It is home to an unequalled display of this ancient rock. The Yavapai County Court House in downtown Prescott is built from the granite. The soils around Prescott are largely of decomposed granite, or *grus*, which, while rather deficient in nutrients, is delightful to walk on, easy to work, and produces little mud. On the other hand, the granite rock is extremely hard, so in order to produce building sites, prodigious amounts of blasting and drilling are often necessary. Most folks feel the expense and time are well worth it.

The "Dells," as they are known locally, pop up and end rather abruptly along U.S. 89. They represent the top of a local pluton. The formations are similar in appearance to those of Texas Canyon, 250 miles to the southeast, but the granites of Texas Canyon are mere infants, only around 52 million years old. Those of Granite Dells are immensely old: somewhere between 1.4 and 1.7 billion years, the same age as the rock found in Granite Mountain, some fifteen miles to the north. That amount of time was necessary to erode away some two miles of material that originally separated the surface from the magma chamber that would become the Granite Dells.

While none of the prominences in the Dells rises more than a couple of hundred feet above its base, they are impossible to ignore. The peculiar weathering process of the granite has rounded the pinnacles and boulders, making for most agreeable climbing, irresistible to young and old. Hiding places also abound, including intimate rock shelters that afford relief from the chilly winds of winter and early spring and the blaze of summer sun. They also offer concealment from unwelcome observers. Granite Dells is home to a couple of small reservoirs that fill occasionally. One of the dams impounds Granite Creek, the major drainage from Prescott.

Fort Whipple is located near the southern entrance to the Dells. It was founded in 1864, primarily as part of the U.S. government's campaign against Indian uprisings. Today it is a veterans' hospital and museum. A small portion of the fort was provided to Yavapai people in 1935 and became the base for the Yavapai Prescott Indian Reservation, which was later greatly expanded.

The Dells are nearly all private property. Until 1956, the only swimming area around Prescott available to the general public was a privately owned pool formed by a dam across a creek within the

Granite Dells, with Granite Mountain in the background.

Granite Dells. While it was an unusually delightful place, sandwiched among enormous granite formations, it bore a sign at the entrance, "We solicit white patronage only." In 1956, a spirited group of Prescott civic leaders raised funds and constructed a pool in the town that was open to all. Admissions to the Dells pool subsequently declined rapidly.

Granite Mountain from the south.

Granite Mountain

PRESCOTT

From Williamson Valley Road and Iron Springs Road north of Prescott and from U.S. 89 to the north of Granite Dells, Granite Mountain looms over the countryside. At an elevation of 7,625 feet (2,325 m), it is one of the high points in the Prescott region, part of a range known as the Sierra Prieta. (That name is known mostly from old maps. I grew up in Prescott and never heard of the Sierra Prieta until I read of it decades later.) A trail leads to the summit. The mountain is included in Granite Mountain Wilderness of Prescott National Forest, and the sheer cliff face on the southwestern side (on the extreme left in the photograph) is popular with daring rock climbers. To the recreationists' disappointment, the cliff is closed each spring to protect a nesting area of peregrine falcons. An impoundment created during the Great Depression has produced a small but very popular lake, campground, and picnic area at the base on the mountain's southern side, part of the Granite Basin Recreation Area. Swimming is prohibited. Perhaps it was in the late 1950s as well. If so, night enforcement in those days was nonexistent or so intermittent that it never bothered me.

As is the case in most of the Prescott area and to the south and west, the rock of the mountain is extremely old—old even for Proterozoic rock. It was raised to more than 10,000 feet during a mountain-building episode called the Yavapai orogeny that took place 1.8–1.7 billion years ago. Geologists have determined that during that lengthy period the clash of tectonic plates weakened the earth's crust and magma intruded, forcing its way into the even older schist, squeezing up a vast pool of magma that failed to reach the surface. Over the following billion years or so magma cooled into granite (or, more properly, granodiorite). Since then the upper couple of miles of surface have eroded or faulted away, leaving the resistant granite exposed. Granite Mountain is the remnant of a very large glob.

Harquahala Mountains, viewed from the southwest. The pinkish layer, seen to the right of the saguaro, clearly tilted, is composed of 330-million-year-old Redwall Limestone of Mississippian age, the same layer that dominates the interior of the upper Grand Canyon and is present throughout the Colorado Plateau, where it lies horizontal. The crest to the far right, which includes the summit at 5,681 feet elevation, is composed of Precambrian gneiss that was exhumed when a massive block that once lay atop slid off to the northeast.

Harquahala Mountains

INTERSTATE 10, SOUTHEASTERN LA PAZ COUNTY

The Harquahala Mountains is perhaps the Sonoran Desert's most impressive purely desert range. Though it is over a mile high (5,681ft, 1,732 m), it is completely surrounded by the desert. Its summit is the highest point in La Paz County and, for that matter, the highest point in southwestern Arizona. For several hundred years, it has functioned as an important marker for desert crossings heading west to California from the Salt River Valley via the ford of the Colorado River at Ehrenburg/Blythe. Its appearance elicited uneasiness, for travelers heading west usually knew that once past the Harquahalas, they were entering very dry desert with scalding summer temperatures and no reliable water until they reached the river eighty miles away. Harry Winters reports that the name Harquahala is derived from the Yavapai name for the range, Ahakwahél, which means "place where the water runs." An ephemeral stream formerly ran along the western end of the range. Overpumping of the regional aquifer for industrial agriculture and the sustained drought of recent decades have caused the stream to dry up completely.

Much of the northern Harquahalas are included in Harquahala Wilderness, an excellent isolated mountain habitat with a wealth of desert fauna and flora. The range might well be considered a sky island, for it harbors several different habitats along with a superb diversity of reptiles, especially rattlesnakes: five species can be found in the mountain complex, I will testify. A trail and even an old jeep trail, still in use, lead to the top, where a century ago the Smithsonian Institution maintained a laboratory studying solar effects. To the north is the wilderness.

Much of the Harquahala Mountains is considered a metamorphic core complex: stretching of the earth's crust caused an earlier cap on the northeastern part of the mountain to slide away as far as 25 miles (40 km) to the northeast along what is called a detachment fault. With the weight of that great mass removed and under pressure from below, the current mountain rose in rebound. A majority of this underlying rock is granodiorite of roughly 1.6 billion years of age. As the fault slid away, this underlying rock was subjected to enormous pressure and became pliable and cooled, forming gneiss. The rock now at the surface reveals the marks of the low-angle faulting action similar to that found in the Santa Catalina Mountains and exhibits the same dome effect. The same activity affected several of the mountain ranges in the vicinity, including the Harcuvars, the next range to the northwest.

A surprising geologic feature of the Harquahalas appears in the western portion, which exhibits the same layer sequence, strongly

Harquahala Mountains in the far distance, as seen from Yarnell Hill to the northeast. Note the dominant size. The dome shape is characteristic of metamorphic core complex mountain ranges in Arizona.

tilted, as that found in the Grand Canyon two hundred miles to the north and in many parts of the Colorado Plateau. The sequence is visible in the photograph on page 85, though the layers have been rotated nearly ninety degrees. Redwall Limestone is especially visible. It lies below the Supai Group, Coconino Sandstone, and Kaibab Limestone, just as in the Grand Canyon. The survival of that sequence in a separate mountain range suggests that this section of the Harquahalas was once part of the plateau. The sequence may constitute a block that remained while the intervening portions of the plateau to the north and east eroded away, similar to Cathedral Rock near Sedona. Rotation would have occurred after separation from the plateau. Another possibility is that the sequence represents a block that broke off and has been ferried southwestward by Basin and Range extension after the detachment fault decapitated the northeastern portion of the original mountain. The geological interpretation is complicated by the apparent presence of outcrops of

Cambrian Bolsa Quartzite, common only in southeastern Arizona. If this identification is correct, mountain elements from the north and the south have converged in the Harquahalas.

Although the Harquahalas exhibit Basin and Range faulting, their composition is different from many other ranges. To the south, east, and southwest, most of the ranges are dominated by volcanic rock. It is largely absent in the Harquahalas, which are closer in composition to the ranges of the Transition Zone to the north and east. The range is well mineralized.

Hat Mountain from Route 85 north of Ajo.

Hat Mountain, Sauceda Mountains
ARIZONA ROUTE 85 NEAR AJO

Hat Mountain is the most conspicuous feature of the Sauceda Mountains. Other peaks are higher, but none can match its unforgettable shape.

The range lies to the east of Arizona Route 85 between Gila Bend and Ajo. *Sauceda* in Spanish means "grove of willows." Harry Winters points out that willows are found at a few "cheepos" or natural water tanks along the eastern end of the range. The name possibly refers to the desert willow, *Chilopsis linearis*, a small desert tree (unrelated to the willow, *sauce* in Spanish) that can survive in dry washes that receive periodic rains. Or, perhaps a Spanish speaker wandering in the bleak countryside of the Saucedas experienced a mirage or hallucination of willow-lined streams of cool water.

Hat Mountain's summit lies at about 2,700 feet (823 m), roughly 1,800 feet above the surrounding desert, and its peculiar shape has made it a landmark for centuries. Most people (though not all) immediately notice that it resembles, well, a hat typical of the nineteenth-century style in northwestern Mexico and the American Southwest. The O'odham name is Vonam Do'ag, which means, logically, Hat Mountain. Others interpret the mountain's shape differently.

The peak is located within the Barry Goldwater Air Force Range; so, while hiking is permitted, one obtains permits (mandatory) with the understanding that potentially being blown to smithereens is part of the deal. The range is strewn with artillery detritus.

The Sauceda Mountains are part of a wildly volcanic area in which geologists have discerned four different periods of volcanism. Hat Mountain is part of the massive outpouring of lava that occurred around 20 MYA, in Miocene times. The peak looks the same from all sides and would require specialized equipment to climb. It is probably the remnant of a crater that filled with lava. The source of lava dried up, and the liquid in the bottom of the crater hardened without ever breaching the crater's rim. Over the intervening millions of years erosion has removed the soft sides of the crater, leaving behind the shape formed by the interior surfaces. The rock is andesite and rhyolite, as is the highly fractured rock featured in the Crater Range, which the highway crosses a few miles north of Ajo.

The terrain in the Saucedas is pockmarked with caves and grottos. Hikers often discover inside them a history of recent human occupation in spite of the Saucedas' location in one of the hottest and driest parts of North America. These articles are usually cast-offs from refugees who have arrived on foot from the south, most of whom are seeking work or safety in the United States. Many of them choose the route through the Saucedas to avoid U.S. Border Patrol checkpoints along highways, even though this entails an arduous trek and the risk of death, primarily from heat stroke or thirst. Temperatures of 115 degrees Fahrenheit are not unusual from June through September.

A few miles southwest of the views of Hat Mountain, Route 85 crosses the eastern end of the Crater Range, where a massive outpouring of 20-million-year-old rhyolites form an impressive band of broken lavas. The rock formations are dikes, masses of magma that forced their way through to or near the surface. Their rock is more resistant than the surrounding country rock, which eroded away, leaving the dikes as testimony to the great eruptions. Hiking within the Crater Range is permitted, but a permit must first be obtained from the headquarters of the Cabeza Prieta National Wildlife Refuge in nearby Ajo.

The ferment of volcanic activity in the region resulted in concentration of metals in ore bodies. One such body, exceptionally rich in copper, proved so important that it gave rise to the New Cornelia mine. The mine opened in 1917 and became one of the richest in Arizona, the first open pit mine in the state. Ajo became a company town, which is how I knew it as a lad. When I was a teenager a friend of mine from Ajo described the herpetofauna from the area in glowing terms, whereby I became hooked on the snakes of Arizona. Ajo endures now as a struggling arts community that burgeons in wintertime with refugees from the frozen north.

Helmet Peak, Sierrita Mountain foothills, Pima County, Arizona.

Helmet Peak, Sierrita Mountains
PIMA COUNTY

Helmet Peak is a limestone *monadnock*, situated about ten miles west of Sahuarita on Interstate 19 in southern Arizona. It rises in a nearly sheer cliff on its west side to the modest height of 3,864 feet (1,178 m). The summit lies only about 400 feet above its base and about 1,000 feet above the Santa Cruz River to the east, but it is a landmark due to its shape. It is now obscured from view from much of the Santa Cruz Valley due to the massive heaps of tailings from open pit mining of copper and molybdenum (among others) that have piled up since the 1960s. The mines are clearly visible from satellites and continue to expand into the surrounding countryside.

The peak itself sits above an ore body that will probably make Helmet Peak expendable. Its similarity to a helmet, the sort that Spanish soldiers wore, suggests it has been a landmark for several hundred years. The name probably stems from the Spanish occupation of the region with its presidio, or fort, at Tubac, some twenty miles to the south of Helmet Peak. The Tubac fortification was founded in 1752 to protect Spanish settlers and religious institutions from Apache attacks. Now the peak is familiar only to cyclists, miners, and the few local residents who frequent Mission Road west of I-19. For bicyclists riding from Tucson, twenty miles or so away, arrival at the peak is a welcome event after a long uphill slog, passing first through the San Xavier District of the Tohono O'odham Nation, past the Mission San Xavier del Bac (W:ak), then along a route through the mines. Access to the peak and lands around it is strictly regulated by the mining interests that control extraction of the minerals. Don't plan to climb it.

Helmet Peak illustrates an unusual structural history. Rather than being a tilted volcanic landmark, as is the case with Picacho Peak, or a volcanic neck or plug, like Agathla, the exposed peak consists of layers of very old (250-plus-million-year-old Permian) Concha Limestone that appears here and there in southern Arizona. The peak appears to be a formation that folded under enormous lateral pressure, until it turned upright, forming the peak. The west side has eroded and collapsed. Imagine pushing a rug until it develops folds. That is analogous to what happened with Helmet Peak. It's an impressive accomplishment of nature.

Hualapai Mountains.

Hualapai Mountains

INTERSTATE 40, NORTHWESTERN ARIZONA

Hualapai Peak towers over the northwestern quadrant of Arizona at a height of 8,417 feet (2,566 m) and rises nearly 6,000 feet from the surrounding plains. The name means "people of the tall pines" in the language of the Hualapai people, whose lands are now mostly to the northeast in the western portion of the Grand Canyon. The peak is the high point of the Hualapai Mountains, a range nearly 50 miles (80 km) long, by far the tallest in northwestern Arizona, and a fine example of Basin and Range block faulting. Lower portions of the range are mostly Mohave Desert, which has cool, sometimes moist winters and hot, dry summers. On the southeastern side, however, the Mohave meets up with the Sonoran Desert, which features hot, moist summers and mild, sometimes moist winters. A sign of these merging deserts is the mingling of the Mohave's Joshua trees with the Sonoran's saguaro cacti, as if the two strangers briefly greet each other but maintain separate territories at their backs. The vegetation of the higher and more northern parts of the range is more like that found in the San Bernardino Mountains of southern California than of the mountains to the south and east in Arizona. The habitats on the mountain resemble those of sky islands of southeastern Arizona, but, unlike them, the higher ones are home to elk. (Around 2015 small numbers of elk appeared on Mount Graham.)

A popular campground represents the only location in western Arizona where humans can easily drive to escape the desert heat and visit pine forests. The closest town of any size is Kingman, the last city on the route west before the descent into the torridly hot Colorado River valley and the Mohave Desert.

Hualapai Peak consists of several distinguishable Proterozoic (or Precambrian, older than 541 million years)—and durable—granites and gneisses, the oldest of which dates from more than 1.7 billion years ago. In much more modern times, perhaps 30 MYA, magma forced its way upward through the ancient rock in parts of the range. Where the molten rock contacted the ancient strata, the magma cooled, and minerals tended to crystallize or settle out, leaving pockets of metal-bearing ore. The Hualapai range is thus riddled with mines, dug by those searching for those pockets.

Kitt Peak (center) and Coyote Mountains (right).

Kitt Peak and Coyote Peak, Quinlan and Coyote Mountains
ARIZONA ROUTE 86

Fifteen miles to the north of Baboquivari Peak in the Quinlan Mountains, separate from the Baboquivaris, Kitt Peak is home to the telescopes of the Kitt Peak National Observatory, an internationally prominent astronomical site. The scopes are located on land leased from the Tohono O'odham Nation. From the summit of Kitt Peak at 6,880 feet (2,097 m), one is awarded a comprehensive view of the Baboquivaris to the south and a host of mountains of southern and central Arizona. The telescopes are often open to the public, but the schedules are restricted.

Kitt Peak with telescope.

Immediately adjacent to the northeast of Kitt Peak and the Quinlans are the Coyote Mountains, capped by Coyote Peak at 6,529 feet
(1,990 m). Though the ranges appear to be connected, they are actu-
ally of quite different origin. The granites of Kitt Peak are roughly
165 million years old, which makes them mid-Jurassic in origin,
older than the Baboquivari Granite. The Coyote Mountains are separated from the Quinlans by a major fault, and the granites there are
late Cretaceous or early Tertiary, about 65 million years old. Coyote
Peak, the high point, appears to be a metamorphic core complex,[§§]
similar in its origins to the Santa Catalina and Pinaleño Mountains,
while the Baboquivari and Quinlan Mountains are not. The rock of
the Coyotes shows signs of ductile/mylonic shear, similar to that
seen in the Santa Catalinas, indicating that a huge mass of rock slid
off as a detachment fault, apparently heading northeast across what
has become the Ajo Highway right-of-way. As it slid, its enormous

[§§] For discussion of metamorphic core complexes, see the Santa Catalina
Mountains entry.

weight caused the partial melting and smearing of the rock immediately beneath the detached portion, producing a rock that geologists call mylonite.

A paved road leads to the summit of Kitt Peak. The grade is a steady 8 percent. Bicyclists I know have been issued citations by the Tohono O'odham Tribal Police for exceeding the speed limit on the descent. As for Coyote Peak, it is not even penetrated by an improved trail. It is nearly inaccessible, even though it is within a wilderness area administered by the Bureau of Land Management. Almost no one climbs Coyote Peak because of the lack of maintained trails and the heavy brush cover that alternates with massive boulders. And access to it lies within the lands of the Tohono O'odham and is their property. Crossing those lands requires their permission.

Kofa Mountains. Photo by Leigh McDonald.

Kofa Mountains, Castle Dome Mountains

NORTH OF INTERSTATE 8, SOUTHWESTERN ARIZONA

The Kofas are the most prominent range in the Yuma area, located north of Interstate 8, east of Arizona Route 95, roughly thirty miles south of Quartzite and Interstate 10. The range is now best known for desert bighorn sheep and the wild desert fan palms (*Washingtonia filifera*) found growing there (and perhaps nowhere else in Arizona). The palms, few in number and drought-stressed, perhaps dead from the searing drought and heat of 2020, can or could be seen growing far up on the mountainside in, appropriately enough, Palm Canyon. That declivity marks the western edge of a caldera that extends nearly four miles to the east.

Kofas are the principal range in the massive (665,000 acres) Kofa National Wildlife Refuge, which was established in 1939 to protect the desert bighorns of the area. It includes the Castle Dome Mountains to the southwest and west of Route 95. By the 1930s desert bighorns were rapidly disappearing due to overhunting, and the Kofa population was remote enough that protection in a refuge seemed the best way to save the bighorn population of southwestern Arizona from extermination. The campaign for protection was led by the Arizona Boy Scouts.

The highest point in the Kofas is Signal Peak, with an elevation of 4,877 feet (1,487 m). It is also the highest point in Yuma County. The summit rises roughly 2,000 feet above the surrounding terrain. Much of the Kofa Mountains is very rough terrain, ideal for desert bighorns, for which concealment is a strategy for survival.

Visitors who hope that "Kofa" is a Native American term for something important will be disappointed to learn that it is merely a shortened form of "King of Arizona," the name of the most important mine in the range. It shut down operations in the 1920s. This is one of the hottest places in Arizona, with summer temperatures exceeding 120 degrees; so whatever our feelings about mining, we must harbor a respect for those tough souls who managed to work the mine for those twenty years.

The terrain of the Kofas gets its roughness from an intense period of volcanic activity between 18 and 23 MYA, a time when all hell was breaking loose every few hundred thousand years or so in much of southwestern Arizona. The basalts, rhyolites, and various tuffs and ash flows are still there to behold. The tortured landscape remains preserved for us, thanks to the low rainfall and humidity in this, the hottest desert in the Southwest.

To the southwest, the Castle Dome Mountains appear as a near mirror image of the Kofas, except that the highest point, Castle Dome, stands out for its distinctive shape. It is a dominant peak at 3,788 feet

Castle Dome Mountains. Photo by Michael J. Miller.

Castle Dome. Photo by Michael J. Miller.

(1,155 m), appropriately named (even though I submit that it looks more like a biscuit than a castle). It is quite visible from the Colorado River, where for centuries it has been an important locator for those living or traveling along the river.¶ The dome is the best-known landmark in far southwestern Arizona. Its O'odham name is Vav Giwulik, the same name assigned to Baboquivari Peak at the eastern end of the Tohono O'odham Nation lands. Castle Dome appears to be the remnant of a resurgent dome that rose from inside a caldera following a catastrophic series of explosions. The age of the volcanism is roughly the same as that of the Kofas, 18–25 MYA.

A famous crossing of the river known as the Castle Dome Crossing was inundated by the waters of Imperial Dam in 1938. The area was mined even more than the Kofas, and a wealth of gold, silver, copper, and lead was extracted long before air-conditioning existed. It even had its own town and, for one year (1875–76), its own post office.

Castle Dome was visible, a landmark, from Fort Yuma, a federal garrison established in the mid-nineteenth century to protect settlers and travelers from rebellious Quechans (Yumas). These native people felt that their land and rights were being stolen by outsiders.

Yuma's air is now beset with haze that makes sightings of Castle Dome from the city unusual or rare.

¶¶ Since the river was dammed in the 1930s and permanent bridges constructed, river traffic has been confined to pleasure boats, a far cry from the steamers and ferries that plied the river in the late nineteenth and early twentieth centuries.

Miller Peak, Huachuca Mountains, slightly left of center, seen from the east.

Miller Peak, Huachuca Mountains
COCHISE COUNTY

The northeastern side of the Huachuca Mountains forms the back-drop for Fort Huachuca and Sierra Vista (formerly Fry), Arizona. The southern edge of the range descends to the border with Mexico. The highest point, Miller Peak, is 9,466 feet (2,885 m) in elevation and rises nearly 5,000 feet above the base of the range. The Huachucas are one of several sky islands, ranges in southern Arizona and New Mexico that are isolated from other ranges and that contain flora and fauna quite different in their higher reaches from what is found at their base. In sky islands, plants and animals more typical of Mexico predominate near the bottom and in the canyons, while at the summits they are similar to those found in colder regimes to the north.

The range is large enough and high enough to harvest rainfall and release it, mostly to the San Pedro River that originates in Mexico and flows from south to north.

On the southeastern foothills of the Huachuca Mountains is Coronado National Memorial. From there, one can look out over the vast plains and foothills of northern Sonora, Mexico, and imagine the hordes of soldiers, Indian assistants, and hangers-on who accompanied the Coronado expedition of 1545. Far more common today are the green and white vehicles of the U.S. Border Patrol. And newly installed walls that will discourage border and wildlife crossing at that point, at least for a few years.

On the northeastern side of the range, Fort Huachuca was established in 1877 as a key base from which the U.S. government engaged Apaches. Since that time, it has had a colorful history and is now a major U.S. military electronics and communications center. Ramsey Canyon, on the northeastern side of the range, is home to a bird sanctuary located in a backdrop of astonishing ecological diversity. Birders flock from all parts of the world hoping to catch a glimpse of species seen almost nowhere else in the United States.

The variety of habitats found in the Huachucas is due its proximity to Mexico and the tropics, and to the complex geology of the range. The rock of the mountains has a deep history of pummeling, twisting, thrusting, and faulting that has produced a convoluted topography and a variety of substrates ranging from Precambrian to Tertiary. The basic structure is derived from Laramide times, probably 80 MYA, but that mass was largely eroded and beveled. When Basin and Range faulting took place, movement among blocks elevated the Huachucas and depressed the San Rafael Valley to the west, a huge swath of grassland so fair and of such majestic proportions that the movie *Oklahoma!* was filmed there in the 1950s.

The complicated structure of the range gives rise to a most complicated geography and a wide range of rock settings. For example, the summit of Miller Peak has a base of quartz monzonite (similar to granite) that was penetrated by volcanic rock, which now overlies it, and which in turn is covered by a small block of limestone, which appears to have been rafted into place by the volcanic rock. To add to the jumble of rock forms, in Jurassic times an enormous volcano erupted in what is now Coronado National Memorial, leaving behind a huge caldera, stirring up a vast amount of rock of different origins and mixing it with lavas and a cover of ash. It's taken a slew of geological detectives to decipher the geology of the Huachucas.

Mingus Mountain, seen from near Tuzigoot National Monument. The summit sits roughly 4,000 feet above Tuzigoot. Photo by Dan Duncan.

Mingus Mountain, Black Hills
CENTRAL ARIZONA

With its highest point at 7,818 feet (2,383 m), Mingus Mountain appears as a lengthy and elevated ridge with a bulge, whether viewed from the northeast or southwest. The mountain's lengthy crest obscures the western horizon when it is viewed from Clarkdale, Cottonwood, or Tuzigoot National Monument in the Verde Valley, 4,500 feet below. The Sinagua people, who lived there a thousand years ago, held it in esteem, especially as a source of lumber and minerals. The mountain is the high point of a long range known simply as the Black Hills. The top offers sufficient flat land to support organized camps and campgrounds. It may have been named after the Mingus brothers, who reportedly ran a sawmill on the crest of the range in the late nineteenth century.

The former mining boomtown of Jerome sits precariously on the north side of the mountain. Driving between Prescott and Sedona, one passes directly through the old town. The mines there yielded millions of tons of copper, much of it high grade, and abundant gold and silver as well, until it closed in 1953, two years before I first visited it. Jerome once had a population of 15,000 and the enviable reputation of being the wickedest town in the west. In 1919, many mine workers of Mexican heritage jointed the Industrial Workers of the World union. They went on strike, protesting low pay and unsafe working conditions. Most of them were kidnapped by vigilantes, loaded into railroad cars, and shipped west. Peace and tranquility returned to the town, and profits to the owners were staggering. After the mines closed in 1953, Jerome became a virtual ghost town. Now, tourists visit the small community of artists living there and redeposit the wealth extracted from the ground.

Mingus is a mesa-like mountain covered with handsome, second-growth pine forests. The temperature there is usually about fifteen degrees cooler than in the Verde Valley to the northeast, and eight degrees cooler than in the Prescott Valley to the southwest. At the extreme northern end lies Sycamore Canyon, whose waters originate in the Mogollon Rim country to the north and whose cliffs offer colors similar to those of Oak Creek Canyon. Portions of the northeastern highlands drop off precipitously into the Verde Valley. As a lad I had the distinct experience of taking in the view there on the very edge from atop a microwave tower on which I was working.

Mingus Mountain consists almost entirely of Precambrian metamorphic rock that was uplifted along a fault while the Verde Valley was downdropped, all within the last 50 million years. The exposures of that ancient rock make Mingus a popular site for geology classes. Its complexity, typical of the Transition Zone, makes the geology of the Grand Canyon appear simple. In several places, far younger lavas cap the ancient Precambrian rock, which has an estimated thickness of 20,000 feet.

Montezuma's Head, Organ Pipe Cactus National Monument, seen from the southwest.

Montezuma's Head and the Ajo Mountains

ORGAN PIPE CACTUS NATIONAL MONUMENT

For miles around, the peak called Montezuma's Head stands out as a solitary knob within a rugged range. It is the most notable prominence in northern Organ Pipe Cactus National Monument, though views of it are often obscured by other crags. The peak, 3,634 feet (1,108 m) at the summit, is held to be noteworthy by the O'odham. Harry Winters reports that its O'odham name is 'Oks Dak, meaning "place where a woman is sitting." The knob at the summit makes it distinctly visible well to the east on the Tohono O'odham Reservation. William Hornaday, leading an expedition through the region in 1908, observed that the "cork-like summit looks absolutely unscalable." It is not. If you feel compelled to climb it, however, reserve your efforts for winter or early spring.

At the base of the peak within the monument, a few organ pipe cacti survive the searing heat and relentless drought. They grow in good numbers elsewhere within the park boundaries, justifying the decision to include the area in the National Park System, but only a few straggling plants exist beyond the park. Outliers reach as far east as the Tucson Mountains. Organ pipe cacti produce fruits sweeter and somewhat more refreshing than those of the saguaro. The plants' limited range within the United States explains the absence of general familiarity with the fruits except among the Tohono O'odham, who for millennia have recognized their virtue.

The Ajo Mountains, of which Montezuma's Head is a part, are volcanic in origin, formed from 17.5 to 16.5 MYA as part of volcanism resulting from the earliest Basin and Range extension. During that period, the land was stretched to the northwest, pulled by a change in direction of the Pacific Plate. Indeed, the thickness of the earth's crust averages about thirty miles outside Basin and Range, but the stretching has thinned it to about sixteen miles within the province.

As the land stretched, sections or blocks broke off and sank, while those on either side rose as they were freed of the weight of the collapsing section. The breaking points were known as faults and made for convenient alleys where, if magma was present, it could work its way to the surface as lava. The flows of Montezuma's Head and that part of the associated Ajo Range and the Saucedo Mountains to the north constitute an excellent example. They are composed of rhyolite, a light-colored lava that, due to its stiff consistency, tends to be associated with explosions rather than spattering and is too thick to form the long flows typical of basalt. Along Estes Canyon to the southwest of Montezuma's Head, deposits of obsidian appear, an indication of lavas that cooled so quickly that crystals did not have time to form. Studies reveal that the rhyolite lava of the peak is at least 1,450 feet thick. Roughly twenty-five miles to the north, Arizona Route 85 crosses a dramatic flow of lava in the Crater Range, dating from the same geological times as Montezuma's Head (see photo, p. 21). The remarkable flow is replete with dikes and diatremes, but to hike off the road requires a permit from the Cabeza Prieta National Wildlife Refuge authorities in Ajo.

Though not especially lofty, the Ajo Mountains are of sufficient size to create a modest rain shadow to the east, leaving a sizeable chunk of the Tohono O'odham Indian reservation slightly drier than that to the west of the range.

Mount Graham from U.S. 70 near Solomonville.

Mount Graham, Pinaleño Mountains

U.S. 70, SAFFORD

At 10,720 feet (3,267 m), Mount Graham stands out as the highest peak in the Pinaleño Range, the highest peak in southern Arizona, and the highest peak of the Sky Island region. It rises more than 8,000 feet from the Safford Valley of the Gila River, making it the Southwest's highest mountain measured from the base. It is a truly colossal mountain system, a dominant mass. Mount Graham was named in 1846 after James Duncan Graham, an officer in the topographic corps that patrolled the northern frontier with Mexico during the U.S. war on Mexico. Local folk refer to the range as "The Grahams."

The Pinaleños are large and high enough to squeeze most water from cyclonic atmospheric storms (winter storms arriving from the west), thus creating a rain shadow, a belt of lowered precipitation to the northeast. Snow on the northern slopes of Mount Graham often remains visible eighty miles to the east until late spring, or at least it did in cooler and clearer times prior to the mid-1990s.

The mountain is sacred to Apaches, with good reason. They arrived in the region in the late seventeenth century, perhaps much earlier, and knew that from the top of Mount Graham much of southeastern Arizona, and often more, is visible, and that the climate is noticeably different at the top than at the base. They were intimately familiar with the variety of habitats and food and fiber resources on the mountain. The northwestern end of the Pinaleños lies not far from the southeastern boundary of the San Carlos Apache Indian Reservation, which was established by the U.S. government in 1872. In the early 1960s I worked on a construction gang near the pass that connects the Pinaleños with the Santa Teresa Mountains to the northwest. In July and August, families of Apaches from San Carlos arrived there to gather acorns of the bellota oak (*Quercus emoryi*). That handsome oak habitat with its sweet acorns was the closest to the San Carlos Apache Indian Reservation.

In the foothills of the western side of the Pinaleños is Fort Grant, established in mid-1872 and later used by federal troops to fight the Apaches. Camp Grant, located nearby, was the scene of an 1871 massacre by vigilantes from Tucson of more than 140 nonviolent Apaches and other Indians, mostly women and children. Survivors were shipped off to Mexico and sold as slaves. Shortly thereafter, Camp Grant was moved to the Fort Grant location.

Because of its isolation from tree cutters, its steepness and ruggedness, and its high elevation, Mount Graham is home to the oldest coniferous trees in the Southwest, especially Douglas firs. A paved highway known as the Swift Trail leads nearly to the top, beginning in desert scrub, then rising abruptly, passing through junipers, then oaks, then pines, then firs and aspen, and finally into a large expanse of spruce-fir at the highest elevation. The five ecological zones on the mountain are the most of any mountain in the United States, some say. The temperature at the summit of Mount Graham is probably about twenty-five degrees Fahrenheit cooler than at Safford. The twisting, steep highway is the site of several bicycle races, very difficult bike races. The University of Arizona has constructed an astronomical observatory at the summit. I attended Boy Scout camp on the mountain in the 1950s at a site called Snow Flat, not far from the summit. It was not flat, and there is almost nowhere on the mountain that is. The Pinaleños are a steep range. Their orientation is typically southeast to northwest, classic Basin and Range.

The Pinaleño Mountains are a good example of what geologists call a metamorphic core complex, similar in origins to the Santa Catalina Mountains (see Santa Catalina entry), where the phenomenon was first described. The dome shape when viewed from a distance suggests their metamorphic core nature. The top is mostly 1.7-billion-year-old Pinal Schist and another Precambrian (more than 541 million years old) rock called Oracle Granite, roughly a metamorphosed granite, in this case nearly 1.4 billion years old, that worked its way into the Pinal Schist. That mass of old earth was uplifted from many miles beneath the surface rather than formed from volcanic explosions, as is the case of the Chiricahua Mountains to the southeast. The uplift is partly the result of the departure around 30 MYA of a huge chunk of rock that once covered the mountain before sliding off at least seven kilometers to the northeast. That colossal mass was loosened by a detachment fault—an immense low-angled fracture that was then pulled downward by gravity, one of at least three such faults in the Pinaleños.

Once the old cap, several miles thick, slid off, the whole remaining mass, buried several miles beneath, was relieved of the weight above.

It gradually rose to the surface, an effect geologists call rebound. Perhaps 15 million years later, as southeast Arizona was stretched from the west, a colossal block broke off from its neighboring crust, rose several miles into the sky, and tilted under Basin and Range extension. An adjacent block to the east also broke off but sank instead and became the basement of the Safford Valley. The rising block became Mount Graham and the Pinaleños. In finding its center of gravity, the block tilted, and rock once buried miles beneath the surface pivoted up to become the summit.

From the Safford Valley on the Gila River, a steeply tilted and eroded mesa near the base of the mountain is clearly visible. That mesa, now cut by channels, is built up from various grades of sediments—clays, silts, sands, gravels, and cobbles—eroded from far above or from upstream. This mass of sediments was once part of the valley floor of the Safford Basin, and the current tilting demonstrates that the valley floor rested on rock that is part of the Mount Graham block and was elevated along with the rest of the mountain as the mass was uplifted and then tilted. Imagine the energy necessary to pull that off.

Mount Turnbull from near Fort Thomas, U.S. 70.

Mount Turnbull

BYLAS, U.S. 70 IN THE GILA RIVER VALLEY

At 8,282 feet (2,524 m), Mount Turnbull towers more than 5,000 feet above the valley of the Gila River west of Safford. It is also usually visible from Globe, forty miles to the west, county seat of Gila County. It is best viewed from the town of Bylas, on the San Carlos Apache Indian Reservation. The peak is part of the Turnbull Mountains, which are usually grouped together with the Santa Teresa Mountains. The Santa Teresa Wilderness, located south of Mount Turnbull, is one of the most inaccessible units of the National Wilderness Preservation System. From the north, access to Mount Turnbull and the Santa Teresas is under the jurisdiction of the San Carlos Indian Reservation, and entrance permits are required of non-Apaches.

From the south one can reach the higher portions of the range only by long and rugged trails that require four-wheel drive to a trailhead or are limited to foot traffic or pack animals. Water is also scarce. This inaccessibility is a godsend for wildlife, which abounds within the Santa Teresa Range.

As a lad I worked on a construction project one summer and camped near the pass that separates the Santa Teresas from the Pinaleños to the southeast. I wondered then about the difficulty of getting into the boulder-strewn slopes to reach the summit. I still wonder. I once hiked a couple of miles up a wash that drains the southeastern side. It was a hot day and the wash was dry. The boulders on the distant mountainside kept receding, at least from my perspective.

From the south and west, the Santa Teresas appear to be made up mostly of granite boulders. These rocks are the result of an intrusion of magma of Oligocene-Miocene age—about 24 MYA—that forced its way through basement rocks more than 1 billion years old. The overlying material between the intruding granite and the surface has since been eroded away, and the tough granite, carved into its distinctive round formations, has come to the surface. The granite formations of the range promise to duplicate the wonders of the Dragoon and Little Dragoon Mountains, but in utter solitude. Mount Turnbull proper consists of a thick layer of rhyolite of roughly the same age, which means that the granite was only a million years or so of age when a period of intense volcanism laid down the rhyolite.

Thanks to magnificent isolation and protection by the Apaches of San Carlos, the Santa Teresas appear little changed from nearly sixty years ago, and Mount Turnbull retains its lofty elegance. The air pollution, however, has changed things.

Navajo Mountain from the southwest. Lake Powell lies mid-photo. Photo by Dan Duncan/ David Yetman.

Navajo Mountain

PAGE, NORTHERN ARIZONA

Geologists call Navajo Mountain a *laccolith*, a domelike rise in the earth's surface produced by pressure of magma from below that has not broken the surface. If the rising magma were to spread horizontally, it would form *sills*. If it rose vertically through cracks, it would form *dikes*. In the case of a laccolith, the rising magma has risen through a sort of tunnel, then flared into a gigantic mushroom shape, forcing the strata above into a dome. With just a little more pressure from magma the top would have been blown off, creating a caldera, as though the earth's mantle had been lanced with a scalpel. A few million years from now erosion will have scraped away the covering layers, revealing the volcanic material, usually granite-type rock.

Navajo Mountain is a textbook laccolith, a dome rising in magnificent isolation. It lies entirely within the Navajo Nation. It is also the highest peak in Navajo lands at about 10,400 feet (3,170 m) in elevation. Hopis, Navajos, Utes, and many Paiutes revere the mountain, which is now off limits to outsiders. While most of its mass is in Utah, its southern flank is in Coconino County, Arizona, so I can claim it for my state. The huge dome, free of competitors, rises from the landscape northeast of Page—its summit is about 6,000 feet above the town—and is visible from much of the Lake Powell area. Excellent views from the northwest are also available from the approach to Rainbow Bridge National Monument in Utah, now accessible primarily from Arizona by boat and a hike from Lake Powell. Although it lies entirely within Navajo lands, Navajo Mountain was home to Anasazi, or Ancestral Pueblo people, centuries before the arrival of Navajos. Hopis, residents of the region for thousands of years, also revere archaeological sites on the mountain and make annual pilgrimages there.

Navajo Mountain has never been easily accessible to visitors. Part of the mountain's mystique lies in the surrounding mesas, buttes, and canyons of the Colorado Plateau that are wildly sculpted. Primitive, arduous trails departing from remote trailheads on Navajo tribal lands pass around its base, leading to Rainbow Bridge. Permits from the Navajo tribe for use of the trails are mandatory, and climbing on the mountain is prohibited. The mountain's status as tribal land and as an object of reverence by indigenous Americans afford Navajo Mountain a greater level of protection from exploiters than exists for landmarks in our National Park System.

The mountain arose, probably about 25 MYA, when a large upwelling of magma surged from the mantle and intruded the many layers of sedimentary rocks (mostly sandstone and limestone) of the Colorado Plateau. The same period of volcanism gave us Agathla, Shiprock in New Mexico, and the Henry Mountains in southeastern

Utah, another example of a laccolith. The magma of Navajo Mountain never managed to reach the surface, but the upward pressure deformed the otherwise flat plateau, pimple-like. The upward force raised the top layer, called Dakota Sandstone, jacking it up nearly 4,000 feet above its original position and the surrounding landscape. The layers beneath the Dakota are still there, though pushed up at an angle, wrapped around the intruding magma like so many blanket edges.

Dakota Sandstone is youthful, as far as the Colorado Plateau sedimentary rock layers are concerned. It is of Cretaceous age, probably less than 100 million years old, younger than the youngest exposed sedimentary rock in the Grand Canyon by about 100 million years.

Picacho Peak from the southeast, Interstate 10. Through the 1960s a beacon illuminated the peak at night.

Picacho Peak and the Picacho Mountains

PINAL COUNTY, INTERSTATE 10

Picacho Peak is perhaps southern Arizona's most prominent landmark, especially so since Interstate 10 passes directly below its summit. From the southeast and northwest Picacho Peak stands out as a solitary sentinel, visible from at least forty miles in each direction, provided it is not obscured by air contaminants. The peak is also an important prominence for the Tohono O'odham, in whose aboriginal lands it was included. The O'odham name is Chemmod, which means its shape is like a giant man pushing against something.

A state park is located at its base just southwest of I-10. That place is important historically, for on April 15, 1862, a Civil War battle was fought below the peak, though the small number of troops involved suggests it was more a skirmish. Confederate troops previously had seized Tucson and hoped to head west and conquer California and its vast gold fields to help finance the War of Secession and protect the institution of slavery. At the battle, Union troops forced Confederates to withdraw and followed them and retook Tucson, perhaps securing California for the Union and preventing the spread of slavery to the western states.

Across I-10 to the north is a continuation of the range, known as the Picacho Mountains, with Neumann Peak as the high point more than a thousand feet higher than Picacho Peak, but seldom noticed. Both the state park and the adjacent mountains contain excellent Sonoran Desert habitat. A trail leads to the top of Picacho Peak (*picacho* means "peak" in Spanish). Although the summit is only 1,500 feet above the base, the trail, which begins on the east side, requires one to cross a saddle and descend on the west side before making the final climb—using cables installed and maintained by the park; so the total elevation gain is more than 2,300 feet. The view from the summit offers a snapshot of the density of traffic along the interstate highway, demonstrating its importance as an east-west artery for travel. The view also affords a perspective on the Central Arizona Project canal, which transports water from the Colorado River to the Tucson area, pumped from an elevation at around 350 feet at the intake near Parker to around 2,700 feet at its final destination. The canal appears as a whitish scar along the base of Neumann Peak to the north.

Picacho Peak's elevation is roughly 3,400 feet (1,036 m), and its rock is of volcanic origin. The high point of the Picacho Mountains, those to the northeast of I-10, is Neumann Peak, just over 4,500 feet (1,372 m) high. That part of the mountains is a collection of granite-like bodies ranging from 1.7-billion-year-old Pinal Schist to late Cretaceous (65-million-year-old) granites. The structure represents what

The Picacho Mountains with Neumann Peak, center.

is known to geologists as a metamorphic core complex (similar to the Pinaleño and the Santa Catalina Mountains), unlike the volcanic composition of Picacho Peak proper.

Although Picacho Peak appears to be similar in its origins to Agathla or Boundary Cone, it is not a volcanic plug. The lavas of the peak, composed primarily of andesite, were emplaced on the Picacho Mountains somewhere around 22 MYA, then appear to have slid off to the south as a detachment fault during Basin and Range extensional tilting, as did the Tucson Mountains, forty miles to the southeast, from their original home on top of the Santa Catalina Mountains. A large block of granite emplaced near the summit of Picacho belies the peak's history. If it were a volcanic plug, that block would not be there. As the lavas of the detachment fault and miscellaneous rock masses picked up along the way were dragged south by gravity and extensional stretching, the huge volcanic mass hung up, probably on some existing resistant country rock, and was rotated upward, much as a random log in a flash flood will suddenly be forced upright when one of its ends snags on debris or an obstacle. Thus, Picacho Peak has been rotated from horizontal to vertical by the stretching of the earth's crust. Meanwhile, the Picacho Mountains, liberated by the removal of the burdensome volcanic cover, rose to their present height, tilted along the way by the block's rotation as it sought its center of gravity. An apparently younger lava flow, perhaps 15 MYA, lies buried in the region, sandwiched between sediments 10,000 feet deep, discovered by deep drilling. It flared briefly, then was buried as the void between Picacho Peak and Neumann Peak filled.

For unknown reasons, the slopes at the eastern base of Picacho Peak seem remarkably attractive to desert wildflowers. In those increasingly rare years with abundant winter or early spring rains, Mexican gold poppies by the millions turn the slopes to a brilliant orange, a powerful tint that is visible from Tucson, forty miles away.

Picketpost Mountain viewed from near Boyce Thompson Arboretum, Superior.

Picketpost Mountain

SUPERIOR, U.S. 60

Just west of Superior on U.S. 60, Picketpost Mountain, a mass of multishaded volcanic rock, stands guard. Its summit is a mere 4,375 feet (1,333 m) above sea level, but it rises 2,000 feet above its base, which makes it a prominent mountain indeed. Though visible for many miles to the north and west, it is best viewed from Boyce Thompson Arboretum, an Arizona state park, the site of the former mining town named Pinal (which means "pine forest" in Spanish). From that point, among a vast array of desert plants, one looks directly upward to the slopes of the peak. The O'odham call the mountain Mo'o 'Ialik, "the place where the head rolled down."

Picketpost Mountain is named for its role in the early 1870s as an observation post for U.S. soldiers hoping to monitor the movements of Apaches, with whom the U.S government was at war. It served later as a heliograph station, a relay in a network of mirrors used to transmit signals in remote regions, using a code to advise of potential conflict. The disputants were usually Indians who were reluctant to turn over their ancestral lands to settlers.

In the early 1900s the town of Pinal was founded and came to house William Boyce Thompson, who amassed fabulous wealth after arranging for the extraction of copper, gold, and silver from nearby mines. Apparently entranced by the majesty and intricacies of Picketpost Mountain, he had a house built on the site of the future arboretum. He also established the arboretum.

The shades of color and the rugged, dissected appearance of Picketpost Mountain are an indication of the variety of volcanic rocks that compose its slopes. Each has a different susceptibility to erosion. Remnants of several volcanic eruptions can be detected on the mountain, each producing material of different volcanic composition, color, texture, and resistance to erosion. One explosion in particular that occurred some 18 MYA is chiefly responsible for its appearance now. The flows from that volcano were of lava called quartz latite, which cools to a most durable rock and has resisted erosion more than the other rocks on the mountain through all these millions of years. The deep forces that created that flow also created the Superstition Mountains ten miles to the north.

The volcanic outpourings that produced Picketpost Mountain were deposited on a base of Precambrian Pinal Schist and, above it, the multilayered Apache Group, best seen in the Salt River Canyon (see Salt River Canyon entry.) The peculiar geological structure created various seeps and springs, assuring a faithful, if not abundant, water supply in the creek at the west side. The orientation of the base made for a warm microclimate. All these combined in a location ideal for a botanical garden. William Boyce Thompson made a wise choice.

Portal Peak seen from Rodeo, New Mexico. The high point is located behind the closest peak.

Portal Peak and Silver Peak, Chiricahua Mountains
NEW MEXICO STATE ROAD 80

If Cochise Head stands out from the mass of the Chiricahuas when viewed from the north, Portal Peak and Silver Peak are the dominant features when the range is viewed from the east in the vicinity of Rodeo, on New Mexico State Road 80. From that vantage point, both peaks obscure the mass of the higher Chiricahua ridge to the west. Portal Peak reaches 8,560 feet (2,609 m), while Silver Peak sits at about 8,000 feet (2,438 m) elevation (accounts differ).

The small town of Portal nestles about 4,000 feet below the peaks at the mouth of Cave Creek Canyon. Cave Creek has stretches of permanent water upstream from Portal as it flows between the peaks.

Silver Peak, Chiricahua Mountains, seen from New Mexico State Road 80 near Rodeo, New Mexico, on the east side of the range.

Silver Peak is a more or less solitary mass to the west of Portal. A steep but popular trail, about nine miles round trip, leads to the top, ending at a concrete block that formerly anchored a fire lookout. Portal Peak rises to the southeast. It has no official trail and is a mass of cliffs and very obstructionist brush covering steep slopes, with only occasional conifers. The thought of climbing it now makes me cringe.

Cave Creek Canyon is a most agreeable place, surrounded by massive rhyolite cliffs and is a graphic reminder of the force and size of the Portal caldera. It is the largest drainage on the east side of the Chiricahuas and one of the few places with reliable stretches of water. Trails from the canyon bottom connect with Chiricahua Wilderness, far above. A maintained roadway follows the creek for a couple of miles, then turns to dirt as it winds sharply upward, traversing steep slopes before crossing the crest of the Chiricahuas and descending into the Sulphur Springs Valley. Snows sometimes force closure of the roadway in wintertime. When I was living in the Chiricahuas in the early 1970s, the driver of a semi tractor-trailer, apparently seeking to avoid the inspection station at the New Mexico state line on Interstate 10, opted to take the roadway across the Chiricahuas. That route appears on most road maps. The rig jackknifed and jammed into a narrow concrete bridge around a sharp curve on the west side. It took crews nearly a week to extricate the twisted mess, during which time the road was closed. I never learned what happened to the driver.

Cave Creek Canyon is renowned for the diversity of its fauna, especially birds and reptiles. Many species of plants and animals more typical of Mexico are resident or visitors here. The remarkable variety of life forms led the American Museum of Natural History in 1955 to establish the Southwestern Research Station, where scientists from around the world carry out research into the natural history of the range and of the plants and animals that reside therein.

Residents of Portal had a most distressing view of the Horseshoe Fire in 2011 that burned about 225,000 acres of heavy forest and brush on the higher mountains, destroying much of one of the few Pleistocene relict coniferous forests (those representing lingering elements of the last ice age) remaining in the Southwest. The fire continued for roughly six weeks, exhaling prodigious quantities of smoke. It was probably human caused. The range is slowly recovering from that conflagration. Parts of the burned area benefited from the thinning of brush and tinder. Other habitats were altered forever. The formerly extensive trail system was heavily damaged. In 2019, eight years after the holocaust and a period of sustained drought, much of the coniferous forest that burned showed few signs of recovery to its former condition. Portal Peak and Silver Peak escaped damage, probably due to their isolation.

Both peaks are composed of volcanic rock, similar in origin to most of the Chiricahuas. Both are derived from an enormous volume of rhyolite deposited when a massive eruption tore the eastern Chiricahuas apart, roughly 27 MYA. That cataclysmic explosion formed the Portal caldera, whose structure becomes apparent when viewed from above, especially after someone has pointed it out. A few hundred thousand or so years later, about 26.5 MYA, the Turkey Creek caldera on the western side of the range exploded, producing the silhouette of the range seen from afar.

Not all the area is of volcanic origin, however. A limestone hill a couple of miles northwest of Portal, probably of exposed (presumably) Mississippian Escabrosa Limestone (about 335 million years old), lies outside the area disrupted by the Portal caldera. It presents a graphic illustration of how vegetation is affected by substrate. A dozen or so plant species appear on that little mountain that are absent from the adjacent volcanic rock and soil.

Portal Peak, left, and Silver Peak, right, seen from the east.
Cave Creek Canyon lies between the peaks.

Ragged Top, Ironwood Forest National Monument, looking from the east.

Ragged Top

INTERSTATE 10 BETWEEN MARANA
AND PICACHO PEAK

The appropriately named Ragged Top reaches 3,611 feet (1,100 m) in elevation, about 1,500 feet above its base. Its O'odham name is Vav Chuuchk, meaning a rock outcropping that occurs in more than one place. Although a good ten miles west of Interstate 10, it occupies a prominent place because of its distinctively rough terrain and irregular silhouette. Ragged Top is situated in Ironwood Forest National Monument, of which it is the landmark. The mountain is an outlier of the Silver Bell Mountains, which are home to an active open pit mine producing an abundance of copper, lead, zinc, and silver. By the mid-1980s the mine had produced 1.3 billion pounds of copper.

The peak's rough summit is thanks to its volcanic history. It consists of rhyolite somewhere between 14 and 30 million years of age, that is, somewhere within the mid-Miocene and mid-Oligocene. (I have not been able to locate any precise dating of its rock.) The rugged peaks are formed from an erosional remnant of volcanic activity from which all less resistant rock has been stripped. It is possibly the remnant of a volcanic plug of great size.

Ironwood Forest National Monument, administered by the Bureau of Land Management, contains important stands of the ironwood tree, *Olneya tesota*, a Sonoran Desert stalwart. These venerable trees grow only in the more frost-free portions of the desert. They seem to have found the vicinity of Ragged Top especially to their liking, for the finest groves of the plants I have seen are found within the protected area. These trees may live more than one thousand years and provide protection and nourishment under their branches to a wide variety of organisms. They are a source of nutritious leaf litter, and through the nitrogen-fixing action of their roots they enrich the soil. Alas, their wood is highly sought after as firewood, hence the value of protection within the monument. Numerous examples of pre-Columbian rock art carved into the desert varnish are protected within the monument as well.

Rincon Mountains from the south. Rincon Peak, center. The rounded mountain to the right is Mica Mountain, slightly higher in elevation.

Rincon Mountains

INTERSTATE 10, TUCSON

The Rincon Mountains lie entirely within the Rincon Mountain District of Saguaro National Park. Rincon Peak, the most visible from Interstate 10, is 8,482 feet (2,585 m) in elevation. The highest point in the Rincons and in the park is Mica Mountain at 8,666 feet (2,655 m), a rounded summit somewhat to the north of Rincon Peak. *Rincón* in Spanish means "inside corner," a reference to the mountains' appearance of providing a protective corner to Tucson's northeast side. Although the park was created originally as a national monument to honor and preserve the saguaro cactus, it goes far beyond that noble aim, preserving and honoring an entire mountain range and ecosystem that is home to a wide array of life zones ranging from

Sonoran Desert in the lower portion to forests of pine and fir in the high country.

In 1905, in a grove of ponderosa pines at one of the few flat spots in the high portions of the range, Levi Manning, a pioneering merchant of Tucson, had a cabin constructed for his family in which to escape the heat of the Sonoran Desert summer. His wife was reportedly in agreement, but apparently on the condition that the cabin be furnished with a piano. The instrument was disassembled and shipped on mules to the top, then reassembled, much, it seems, to Ms. Manning's contentment. Or so the story goes. The site is now called Manning Camp. It is a public campground and residential site for park workers but is accessible only by a lengthy trail beginning far below in the desert, one of a number of trails that crisscross the range. I will testify that a marvelous trail connects the north side of the Rincons with the south side and leads from saguaro cacti to pines and back down to saguaros over a space of more than twenty miles. Trails are a necessity due to the rough topography and often unfriendly vegetation. I once joined some friends hoping to scale Rincon Peak by bushwhacking up the eastern side, which drains into the San Pedro River. We failed.

The saguaro cactus population of the Rincon Mountain District of Saguaro National Park is much reduced from the numbers found there in the 1930s when the monument was created. The decrease in the numbers of the giant cacti was due to the death of many giants from old age and the general failure of recruitment of replacements, caused, in turn, by a variety of environmental and human factors. The numbers have recovered somewhat, but not with the density of one hundred years ago. The Tucson Mountain District of the park, however, located in the Tucson Mountains to the west of I-10, harbors forests of millions of the plants in a variety of ages.

Much of the surface rock of the Rincon Mountains consists of a mixture of granites and the metamorphic rock known as gneiss. The latter is exposed in a surface called mylonite, a mineral of fine, often sparkling grain that is produced when coarse rocks such as granite are subjected to a combination of immense pressure, heat, and shearing such as occurred when a huge mass slid off the mountain. That occurred some 30 MYA, a phenomenon called a detachment fault, the same fault that denuded the Santa Catalina Mountains to the northwest. The dominant rock, which becomes most familiar to those hiking in the Rincons and in the nearby Catalinas, is 1.4-billion-year-old Oracle Granite, but a complex assemblage of more recent granites combines with the Oracle Granite, producing a confusing surface. The same forces that produced the modern Santa Catalina Mountains gave us the Rincons.

The National Park Service maintains a visitor center and some fine roadways in the western part of the park. The remainder, including the high country, is wilderness. One can hike in those parts for many hours without encountering another human being. Or water.

Salt River Canyon from Arizona Route 77. The cliff formation is Dripping Springs Quartzite, dated at about 1.15 billion years of age, intruded by the darker lavas, below.

Salt River Canyon

ARIZONA ROUTE 77

The great rift in the earth we call the Salt River Canyon is hardly a landmark in the sense of a prominence. Yet it is a spectacular feature of the landscape, appearing quite suddenly to the traveler, producing an unforgettable panorama, a textbook on geological history, and a view of the innards of Arizona's Transition Zone. A bridge crosses the Salt River, permitting a brief glimpse of the canyon's rocky bottom. The river's current alternates between rapids and stretches of calm. It appears to have followed a great fault crack in the earth's surface while carving its way into the tough rock. Formations of the canyon walls when viewed from below are truly monumental.

On Arizona Route 77 between Globe and Show Low, the roadway drops abruptly from a rolling plateau onto a cliff face. Layers of different rock merge, sometimes sharply, as switchbacks cut through a sequence of geological history. These rocks were already ancient when the layers of the Grand Canyon were youthful.

The canyon sections at the crossing and to the east lie inside the White Mountain Apache Reservation (formerly Fort Apache Indian Reservation). At least one thousand years ago these lands were home to Sinagua people, who left behind signs of their way of life. To the west is the Salt River Wilderness within Tonto National Forest. The river there winds through a rugged series of canyons and peaks of volcanic origin. Within this convoluted terrain, the river landscape includes some challenging white water and has become a popular raft journey and an outdoor classroom for geologists. River trips put in just downstream from the bridge and arrive at Roosevelt Lake five days and fifty-two miles later.

The Salt River begins where the White River and Black River join far upstream. They drain much of the White Mountains, forming the largest river originating in Arizona and the primary source of water for the Salt River Valley in which Phoenix is located. Salt formations downstream from the bridge give the river its name. In drought years, such as the year when the photo was taken, it is much reduced in volume.

The rocks seen from the highway as it descends and ascends the canyon walls consist of Precambrian layers, the oldest about 1.3 billion years old. Most interesting are the masses of dark rock that appear between the more colorful strata, the sequence of which is called the Apache Group. The layers are referred to as a group, since they appear together and in the same order throughout the region, well into southern and central Arizona.

The dark rock layer is lava, the hardened remnants of magma that squeezed its way into sills, moving horizontally after forcing its way upward through the weak spots in the existing country rock. Probing the overlying rock, it found or created channels parallel to the existing layers. The stupendous pressure from the magma pried opened these layers as the lava worked its way into the existing formation and forced the layers apart, sometimes prying them open and creating intrusions of the lava hundreds of feet thick. Most of the dark lava appears within the pinkish formation known as Dripping Springs Quartzite, a durable rock laid down at the edge of ancient seas, visible in this photograph. The lavas spurted through that formation about 1.15 billion years ago, which shows that the quartzite must be far older.

Lavas also penetrated the Mescal Limestone, which forms the white to gray thick layer above the Dripping Springs Quartzite but is not clearly visible here. This same sequence of the Apache Group ancient rock underlies much of east-central Arizona and even extends south to the Santa Catalina Mountains near Tucson.

Dripping Springs Quartzite is named after a mountain range to the south. Mescal Limestone is named for a range in the same vicinity. Although the quartzite is a most durable rock, in places it is less dense and subject to undercutting, thus producing caves and grottos. The Mescal Limestone above is a sturdy, enduring rock, strong enough that thousands of blocks of it were carved to construct Theodore Roosevelt Dam in 1911 downstream on the Salt River. The dam holds back the principal water supply for the Salt River Valley. The original structure has now been encased in concrete. No fault of the Mescal Limestone.

San Francisco Peaks. Photo by Dan Duncan.

San Francisco Peaks

INTERSTATE 40, NORTHERN ARIZONA

The Peaks, as the San Francisco Peaks are locally called, are an extinct stratovolcano. They are Arizona's tallest mountains and dominate the landscape for a hundred miles in all directions. They define the Flagstaff area. As a lad growing up in Prescott, eighty miles distant, I had a clear view of the peaks from my classroom windows and could monitor the amount of snow they accumulated. Humphreys Peak, the high point, reaches 12,635 feet (3,851 m) above sea level, or thereabouts, about 5,700 feet above the base of the mountains at Flagstaff. The peaks are considered sacred by Havasupais, Hopis, Navajos, Zunis, and several other indigenous groups. Each group has a distinct characterization of the history and meaning of the peaks. Some Navajos, whose reservation is closest to the range, refer to the peaks as Abalone Shell Mountain. The mountains were surely viewed with awe and reverence by the Sinagua people, who constructed the building complex at Wupatki National Monument about a thousand years ago. The peaks also contain the only true alpine habitat in Arizona, creating a home for tundra-adapted plants. Among the trees that survive near timberline is a Rocky Mountain bristlecone pine more than 2,600 years old.

Snowmelt and rain sequestered by the peaks are the source of Flagstaff's municipal water supply. This free water is a boon to the city, for it sits on porous layers of rock strata of the Colorado Plateau that preclude the formation of streams. As the climate has warmed and snows become less frequent, authorities have warned the city of impending water deficits.

The Snow Bowl is Arizona's highest, most reliable, and most popular ski resort. It is situated at 9,200 feet, and its highest lift reaches above 11,000 feet, meaning that its presence on the mountain is noticeable from afar. Its existence and operations have offended several indigenous American groups who view the mountain as sacred. Early Catholic missionary priests named the peaks in honor of Saint Francis.

Geologists agree that the peaks were once several thousand feet higher, probably between 15,000 and 16,000 feet. About 1.4 MYA the original volcano began erupting at the plateau's surface and the mountain began to grow as successive lava flows built on each earlier flow. Some geologists believe that perhaps a half million years ago a catastrophic explosion blew off the top, the sort of blowout that occurred in 1980 on Mount St. Helens, Washington, on a far smaller scale. The explosion would have produced the caldera, a semi-crater in the interior of the mountain, and reduced its height by at least 3,000 feet. A subsequent and more popular explanation for the crater-shaped interior is that a truly massive debris landslide, the type that geologists call *mass wasting*, occurred. It would have been an earthshaking movement when billions of tons of volcanic matter slid to the northeast, leaving behind the crater-shaped valley and depositing the enormous mass in the flatter country downhill. The landslide was not associated with volcanic activity, hence is known as a *cold debris flow*.

A couple of hundred thousand years of erosion and glacial scraping has further reduced the mountains' size and shaped the valley within a partial circle of peaks. It is the only mountain in Arizona clearly shaped by glaciers. Today there are several peaks, rather than the single summit of pre-decapitation times. Within the valley is a smaller mountain, known as Sugarloaf Peak. It is a volcanic dome that formed about 50,000 years ago, long after the debris flow (or explosive beheading) created the central valley.

Santa Catalina Mountains. Tucson, with Santa Catalina Mountains in the background.

Santa Catalina Mountains, Mount Lemmon, Pusch Ridge

INTERSTATE IO, TUCSON

The imposing Santa Catalina Mountains, with a domelike silhouette when viewed from afar, define the Tucson area landscape. From Interstate 10 the range appears to be a lengthy uplift of mountains that parallels the northern reaches of the highway southeast to northwest, a classic Basin and Range orientation. The peculiar geological history of the range has resulted in a dome shape rather than a knife-edge summit as is the case with some of the Catalinas' neighbors. This dome effect has resulted in some relatively flat expanses in the high, forested country, making for a wide variety of recreational opportunities.

The high point of the Catalinas is Mount Lemmon at 9,157 feet (2,791 m). It is named for Sara Lemmon, a botanist who roamed the range and described the flora in the 1880s. The size of the range and their height make them vital to Tucson's existence: their slopes intercept rainclouds and trap and collect rain and snow, releasing water that helps replenish Tucson's aquifer. They alter the regional climate by providing habitats that have become classic representations of islands in the Sonoran Desert, gradations of life zones that change with altitude, as Sara Lemmon discovered. And the Catalinas are the principal destination for multitudes seeking snow in the winter or a reprieve from the heat in summer. As the Southwest has warmed, snows in the late twentieth century and first decades of the twenty-first century have been generally inadequate to provide for high-quality skiing, but lifts at Ski Valley, near the summit, await with enduring hope for a blanket of powder in cold weather.

A small, populated area called Summerhaven is located at the terminus of the Mount Lemmon highway near the top of the mountain. This wildly popular paved highway, also known as the General Hitchcock Highway (after a U.S. postmaster general) or the Catalina Highway, winds through massive outcrops of light-and-dark-layered gneiss, followed by granite-derived boulders and bizarre formations called *hoodoos*, for more than twenty-five miles from the base. Begun in 1933 and completed in 1950, the route has become a nationally prominent bicycle destination. The base of the mountain is saguaro-rich Sonoran Desert. Summerhaven is situated in a mixed-conifer forest of pine, fur, and spruce, most of which burned off in a massive fire in 2003. A second fire in 2020 burned large portions of the range that had escaped the 2003 holocaust. From Summerhaven the popular Wonderland of Rocks trail leads into a maze of boulders and forests. From near Summerhaven, one may coast to the base on a bicycle for nearly twenty-five miles, often at speeds that reach foolhardy limits. Sheriff's deputies routinely ticket cyclists for speeding.

Fifty-million-year-old Wilderness Granite of Pusch Ridge Cliffs, Santa Catalina Mountains. Photo by Dan Duncan/David Yetman.

Sabino Canyon, a major drainage on the southeast side of the range and home to a perennial stream, drains the Mount Lemmon area. The lower canyon has become a nationally recognized site for observing plants and birds of the desert and a desert stream. Shuttle vehicles deposit, and retrieve, passengers well into the canyon to trailheads that lead upward into the coniferous forests of the higher country.

The Santa Catalinas are an important example of a metamorphic core complex, joining Mount Graham in the Pinaleños and the Rincon, Picacho, and Harquahala Mountains, among others. Geologists in general had difficulty in explaining the geological nature of the range until late in the twentieth century, and the Santa Catalinas were the range in which most of them carried out their studies of metamorphic core complexes. Most geologists now agree that 70 million years or so ago, a large volcano erupted on top of what is now the Santa Catalinas, atop a thick base of granite roughly 1.4 billion years old. At that time the granite, called Oracle Granite, was buried some seven miles deep in the earth's crust. A colossal explosion created a caldera (crater) as much as twenty miles across atop the existing terrain. There the volcanic mass sat for nearly 40 million years. The theory proposes that about 30 MYA, due to stretching of the crust and massive amounts of heat from below, the volcanic portion broke off and slid, caldera and all, to the southwest (relative to the remaining mass of the mountains). The mechanism along which it slid is called a *detachment fault*, a low-angled fracture moving the mass that was six to eight miles thick. After about 15 million years of infinitesimally slow creep, the volcanic array reached more or less its current location, roughly eighteen miles from its origin. The immense weight of the volcanic mass and the heat generated by the sliding of the fault softened, melted, and pulled the rock beneath. This titanic action and the immense heat it generated produced a characteristic appearance of stretching, smearing, and smoothing of the rock beneath the fault, which is today widely evident in both the Santa Catalina and Rincon Mountains. With the weight above the fault removed and heat from below providing buoyancy, the great mass of rock that remained shrugged off its former burden and rebounded, that is, rose to the surface and above to become the range we now see—an enormous mass of metamorphic rock mixed with granite.

The volcanic mass may have become the Tucson Mountains, west of the Santa Cruz River. It is usual with detachment faults for the sliding, detaching upper layer to become shattered, broken, and chaotic, as I explain in the Tucson Mountains entry. The layer beneath the fault stays in place, remaining comparatively smooth and stretched, rather than broken. The rock left behind, called mylonite, has been altered by the tremendous heat generated by the fault movement that made the rock flow like plastic.

Visitors driving up the Mount Lemmon highway have an unusual opportunity to see up close the resulting gneiss—granites of varying ages seen in layers that have been subjected to colossal pressure, heat, and smearing. That gneiss, attractively layered with black, gray, and brown, and often laced with mica, forms the rock nearly all the distance from the base to Milepost 5 on the Catalina Highway. With a little imagination, it is possible to envision a huge rock mass inching downhill above the exposed rock, producing evidence of its flow in the underlying layers.

The Catalinas consist mostly of granites of varying age—from 1.4 billion years to a mere 27 million years old—that have experienced a wide range of heat and pressure. Perhaps the best view of the younger granites of the range is of Pusch Ridge viewed from the northwest side in Oro Valley. From here the rather young—50-million-year-old—Wilderness Granite forms sheer, whitish cliffs in a most dramatic fashion.

Geologists explain the varying ages of granite within the Catalinas thus: The 1.4-billion-year-old Oracle Granite remained deeply implanted for more than one billion years after its original emplacement—an enormous pluton. During the Laramide orogeny (roughly 40–80 MYA), plate movements activated ancient faults and through them sent magma upward toward the Oracle Granite. The immense amount of heat melted large portions of the Oracle Granite, and the resulting liquid oozed upward in various directions where it cooled into a new form of granite, often mixing with the older rock. This activity occurred several times, producing granites of varying ages throughout the Catalinas, all derived from the ancient and original Oracle Granite. And all thanks to the Laramide orogeny. The movement of the detachment fault later deformed much of the upper granite.

Santa Rita Mountains. Mount Wrightson is at center. Mount Hopkins is capped by the white telescope building. Elephant Head is the granite monolith.

Santa Rita Mountains

INTERSTATE 19

From Interstate 19 south of Tucson, Mount Wrightson (occasionally spelled "Wrightston") to the east is the tallest peak visible, at 9,453 feet (2,881 m). The Santa Cruz River (now an ephemeral stream) separates the Santa Ritas from the mountains to the west—the gentle Sierrita Range to the northwest and the rugged Tumacácoris to the southwest. The Santa Cruz River valley is part of a graben, a large block of crustal rock that sank as the crust was stretched and a chunk broke off and dropped into the growing void over the last 15 million years or so. Since then the large hollow created by the fallen graben has filled with sediments thousands of feet thick, and the stream runs through the graben, or it did before the springs and flow were pumped dry.

This was O'odham country, Sobaípuris, as they were originally known by early seventeenth-century Spanish explorers. Spaniards later came to call them Pimas or, even later, Papagos. In the later twentieth century they finally became publicly identified with their name for themselves, the Sobaípuri people of the Santa Cruz and San Pedro Rivers, and Tohono O'odham, the Desert People of the Sonoran Desert, to the north and west. By the late seventeenth and early eighteenth centuries, Apaches had become horse people and arrived from the plains to the east. They established themselves as highly successful hunters, gatherers, and, from time to time, raiders of more settled peoples and frequent enemies of the O'odham.

On the eastern side of the Santa Ritas, near Arizona Route 85, is the site of Fort Crittenden, a historical reminder of the fierce attacks by Apaches on Mexican, O'odham, and U.S. settlers. Just east of I-19, Tumacácori Mission, which dates back to the late seventeenth century, is now a national historic park. The mission has long witnessed the arrival of Europeans in the Santa Cruz valley and their attempts, failures, and successes at colonizing (appropriating) O'odham lands.

In 1752, Spaniards constructed a presidio, that is, an officially designated fort at Tubac, specifically to afford protection to settlers from Apache attacks. They recruited other indigenous peoples to act as ground troops. Later the fort was moved to Tucson.

An excellent, though strenuous trail system provides two routes to the top of Mount Wrightson from the west side. Trailheads take off from Madera Canyon, a principal, northward-flowing drainage in the western Santa Ritas, which is accessible via a paved road from Green Valley and ends at a popular picnicking site. Madera Canyon is renowned for its variety of birds and summer flowers. U.S. Forest Service officials from time to time warn of bears on the trail that departs the canyon en route to the top of Mount Wrightson. Even more hazardous are the semi-feral goats—sternly horned bucks that during rutting season become aggressive toward any creature that moves.

The peak nearer to I-19, that with white buildings on the summit, is Mount Hopkins, elevation 8,553 feet (2,607 m). The buildings are the Fred Lawrence Whipple Observatory, owned and operated by the Smithsonian Astrophysical Observatory. A road reaches the top but is limited to observatory personnel. The area is also popular with mountain bicyclists.

The towering peak Mount Wrightson, the highest in the Santa Rita Range, consists of volcanics over 100 million years old sitting on top of even older rock. If you set out traveling due west from the Santa Cruz valley below Mount Wrightson, you will not encounter a higher mountain until somewhere in the western interior of China. The Santa Ritas are a complex mixture of igneous, metamorphic, and sedimentary rocks of a great variety of ages and origins, ranging from Precambrian to Holocene—that is, ancient to rather young. Geologists love the range because nearly every geological age is represented somewhere readily accessible. In addition, the Santa Ritas are a textbook example of Basin and Range block faulting.

The range is heavily mineralized, as shown by the enormous mountains of mine tailings and other mining operations on the west side of the Santa Cruz valley. To the north and east open mining is visible. Even more is planned.

Elephant Head, the prominent bare peak on the northwestern side, is nearly entirely quartz monzonite, a rock similar to granite, of late Cretaceous age (about 70 MYA). It was probably a plutonic mass, a glob of magma, that forced its way from the earth's mantle into a massive bubble-like chamber, but never reached the surface. During Basin and Range extension, it was tilted on its side and slowly appeared above the land's surface as the elements scratched away at the surface and transported the leavings to the Santa Cruz River channel. Elephant Head is popular with rock climbers.

Close-up of Elephant Head.

On the west side of I-19, the history of mining and continuing extraction operations is evident. The enormous mountains of tailings continue to expand and threaten to engulf much of the remaining landscape.

Sentinel Peak, also known as "A" Mountain, with Tumamoc Hill to the right. Right of center in the background is Cat Mountain in the Tucson Mountains.

Sentinel Peak-Tumamoc Hill

TUCSON

Sentinel Peak is a small mountain geologically connected to the larger and taller Tumamoc Hill to the northwest. The entire mass is composed of volcanic rock. The peak overlooks the Santa Cruz River to the southwest of downtown Tucson. Sentinel Peak and the larger Tumamoc Hill are geologically separate from the larger Tucson Mountains to the west. People have been living on and around the hills for at least four thousand years. The name Sentinel Peak is derived from its function for centuries as an observation point, perhaps for the pre-Columbian Hohokam scouts, probably as well for soldiers from the Spanish presidio founded across the Santa Cruz River in 1775. The peak is better known in Tucson as "A" Mountain, dubbed so after University of Arizona students constructed a large A on the mountain's east face near the summit in 1915. It is a municipal park, and its summit offers commanding views of the city to the east. For decades the parking lot at the summit was best known as a lane of love.

The basaltic rock from its base—roughly 20 million years old—proved ideal for construction. Older portions of the University of Arizona and numerous houses in the area still have walls built from the basalts of Sentinel Peak. The remnants of a large quarry remain on the northeastern base, visible to the left of center in the lower portion of the photograph.

To the northwest, Sentinel Peak is connected by a ridge to the taller and larger Tumamoc Hill, of the same volcanic origin. The word *tumamoc* in the O'odham language means "regal horned lizard," a species of the "horned toad" lizard genus. The mountain is the location of the Desert Laboratory. Now a part of the University of Arizona, it was founded in 1906 by the Carnegie Foundation and was the first permanent institution devoted to research on the natural history of the Sonoran Desert. And it was research in the Desert Lab that led to the creation of Saguaro National Monument, twenty miles to the east, in 1934. Permanent study plots on the mountainsides have provided an outdoor laboratory for over a century. By monitoring those plots over the decades researchers have documented the rates of growth of saguaros and many other desert plant species and charted climatic change in the Sonoran Desert region. The narrow and steep roadway leading up Tumamoc Hill to the Desert Laboratory has become wildly popular with hikers and walkers.

Tumamoc Hill is home to numerous remnants of the Trincheras culture, a mysterious people who lived and farmed at the base and on the sides of the mountain but disappeared around 1,300 years ago. They, the later O'odham, and Spanish settlers and their protectors all benefited from the availability of water from the Santa Cruz, now dry except during floods. Trincheras are terraces, and the hill abounds with them. They trapped rain runoff and soil, making small gardens possible. The dark volcanic rock also absorbed heat, protecting plants from frost during the winter months,

In the last four decades, the slopes of both Sentinel Peak and Tumamoc Hill have become infested with buffelgrass, an invasive African species that flourishes with fire. It now imparts a dull yellow or light brown sheen to both peaks. With rain, the grass turns green and grows rapidly, then dries. The fine growth of saguaros on the slopes seems irrevocably fated to be consumed by fire-fueled buffelgrass. Fire invariably kills most plants of the Sonoran Desert.

Steins Mountain, Interstate 10, Arizona–New Mexico border. The mountain appears to be the flank of a caldera left by a volcanic explosion.

Steins Mountain

INTERSTATE 10, NEW MEXICO

Steins Mountain is only 5,715 feet (1,742 m) high and rises just over 1,000 feet from its base, yet it is a true landmark, visible for many miles. It is notably prominent along the corridor of Interstate 10 at the Arizona–New Mexico border. Although technically in New Mexico, it has served as a landmark for those headed to Arizona and points west since the arrival of Europeans in the eighteenth century and probably long before that. The peak that towers above the interstate highway is also called Quarry Peak, while the name "Steins Mountain" is sometimes reserved for the taller peak to the north.

The mountain, and the ghost town that sits across the Southern Pacific Railroad to the southeast (immediately north of I-10), is named after a Captain (or Major) Steins who was perhaps killed around 1870 in a battle with Apaches or may have lived to a riper age. Take your pick. The name is pronounced "Steens." The ghost town of Steins was associated with the railroad and with mining in the region. A road to an abandoned mine exists on the lower mountainside, ending abruptly. Various attempts to resuscitate the settlement as a tourist stop have failed, largely, it seems, because water must be trucked in and because the site seems more attractive to vandals than to sightseers. The mystique of a ghost town seems to be diluted by the large letters FUMIGATION painted on a semitrailer that has lingered in the old place for more than a decade.

The peak and the cliff-like hill adjacent to the freeway are composed of volcanic tuff, the heritage of lengthy deposition of volcanic ash so heavy that it formed a cement. The entire mountain is probably the remnants of a volcanic dome from which the less durable material has eroded. It may be the edge of a resurgent dome that rose from the ruins of an explosive caldera.

Steins Mountain lies roughly in the middle of the Peloncillo Mountains, a long, rather crescent-shaped range, whose profile is largely due to volcanic activity, much of it within the last 34 million years. The range extends from the Mexican border north to the Gila River. Ash Peak, about twenty miles to the northwest (see Ash Peak entry), is a northern outlier of the same range. Convoluted and eroded remnants of calderas, resurgent and faulted domes, and massive deposits of tuff are clearly visible to the north as I-10 enters Arizona. Much of that labyrinth of rock is protected in the Peloncillo Mountains Wilderness.

The vast playas, or seasonally dry lake beds, to the east are remnants of an enormous basin lake that once drained northward into the Gila River. The playas now have no outlet. Runoff water from the Peloncillos and the nearby Burro Mountains in New Mexico collects in the huge playa and often manufactures satisfying mirages that provoke arguments about the nature of reality. The summit of Cochise Head in Chiricahua National Monument to the southwest provides a landmark to the west. Even farther west appear the Dos Cabezas, which cap the range of the same name.

Sunset Crater. The huge lava flow emerging from the base appears much younger than its nine hundred plus years. Photo by Dan Duncan.

Sunset Crater

FLAGSTAFF

In 1085 CE or thereabouts—a half million years or so after the nearby San Francisco Peaks last exploded—a small puff of ash issued from a fissure in the ground. Over the following days, the fissure expanded, probably quickly, reaching about six miles in length, issuing lava fountains and copious quantities of ash and gases along its length. Within a short time, according to research published in early 2021, a volcanic explosion similar in size to the eruption of Mount St. Helens shook the land for many miles in all directions. Pyroclastic flows of superheated ash and gases and voluminous clouds of ash rose as high as twenty miles into the sky. Gases and ash invaded the countryside at huge speed, blanketing the region with a volcanic deposit known as tephra—a combination of small rocks and ash. At some point, the eruptive activity became confined to a single location in the San Francisco volcanic field. Clouds of ash continued to pour from the site, and fiery ejections of rock fragments built a cinder cone. Lava flows issued from the flank of the cone. How long the eruption lasted is still debated, but it was probably no more than a couple of decades.

The birth of Sunset Crater was thus somewhat different from that of Parícutin volcano in Michoacán, Mexico, which appeared in a cornfield in 1943 and within a few months grew to about 1,400 feet above its base. The new volcano spewed ash and cinders over a broadening area, including pueblos of indigenous Americans. Huge flows of lava engulfed the nearby village and flowed through its church. Within twenty years it went dormant. While it issued enormous volumes of smoke and ash, it never belched pyroclastic flows.

In addition to the violent explosion and the lengthy fissure, Sunset Crater gave birth to lava flows of basalt, one of them more than six miles in length. These issued from the sides of the expanding hill, and large volumes of ash, pumice, rock, and plumes continued to issue from the summit. The combined pyroclastic flows and ash clouds from the new volcano ultimately smothered an area more than 772 square miles (2,000 sq. km) with tephra and probably suffocated most crops being grown in that area, caused roofs to collapse, and produced general disruption of native peoples' lives. Parícutin affected a similar area, causing hardships among native farmers while lava flows destroyed the town. Residents near Parícutin and Sunset Crater were fortunate that the lavas were basaltic, which tend to flow more slowly than humans can walk, rather than rhyolitic, which tend to explode. The latter could easily have obliterated human life in a wide swath of northern Arizona and Michoacán. Just how the basalts of Sunset Crater were involved in an explosive eruption is under investigation.

Especially hard hit would have been those who lived near the new Sunset Crater. The disruption led some of them to relocate to what is now Wupatki National Monument, roughly twenty miles away, which was founded in 1150 CE. By that time the settlers, Ancestral Puebloans now called Sinagua people, must have viewed the volcano as sufficiently subdued to permit construction of a host of new buildings without the threat of being inundated with ash falls. And they discovered, to their delight, that the thick ash held moisture quite nicely and produced excellent yields of corn and squash.

Sunset Crater National Monument, created by presidential decree in 1934, now includes the surrounding countryside, which a millennium later still shows the devastation from this rather small volcano. The National Park Service maintains paved roads and excellent trails (though the summit is not accessible) that give visitors an intimate understanding of the mechanics of how the mountain and crater came to be.

While imaginative descriptions abound of the effects of the crater on native peoples, we need to keep in mind that more than four hundred such craters and lava flows, some of them immense, dot the volcanic field; so people living in the vicinity were aware that the land they had chosen to live in was not a calm landscape, even though none of them had ever seen a volcano in that area. A volcanic eruption and lava flow at Little Springs in the Uinkaret volcanic field a hundred miles to the northwest near the North Rim of the Grand Canyon, however, may be of roughly the same age. Native peoples were probably aware of it and its effects as well, if only through oral tradition.

While we may wonder if Sunset Crater will one day erupt again, such cinder cones usually represent a single occurrence, with spectacular appearance, growth, and effects, followed by dormancy, then extinction. The rather soft cinders of the cone will slowly disappear, and the crater will be rounded off until it becomes just another bump on the landscape. Whether or not a plug will be excavated over the next few million years remains to be seen.

Superstition Mountain viewed from the west. This mountain complex of explosive origin is the most prominent feature of the eastern Salt River valley.

Superstition Mountain
EASTERN MARICOPA COUNTY

I will never forget my first glimpse of Superstition Mountain when I rode from eastern Arizona to Phoenix in the mid-1950s. (Technically, Superstition Range is the name of the famous formation at the western end of the range.) I thought the rugged formation resembled a great battleship, and the entire mountain range had an air of mystery. The Superstition Mountains were known as home to a succession of Native American peoples, who left behind a variety of intriguing rock art and built dwellings within grottos inside the range. The O'odham name for the western end of the range is Vi'ikam Gokodk, meaning "survivor gokodk." As Harry Winters explains, *gokodk* means an uneven, irregular, rough shape.

"Survivor" refers to those who were not drowned in a legendary flood.

The mountains are also notorious for being the supposed location of a fabulously rich lost mine. Somewhere within the forbidding landscape, the famed or fabled Lost Dutchman Mine with its treasure trove of gold remains to be rediscovered. Perhaps. The legend is promoted by numerous developments and businesses in the adjacent town of Apache Junction and the city of Mesa. Prospectors, supposedly by the thousands, still experience the lure of the legendary lost mine. Many are those who venture in search of gold even in the fiery heat of summer. Historical documentation of the fabled mine is vague and imprecise. Maps (available for purchase—no refunds) of questionable authenticity and even more questionable ambiguity abound. Prospectors often view these impediments as mere inconveniences.

Superstition Mountain is part of the Superstition Wilderness, the most visited in Arizona. The U.S. Forest Service lists forty-six trails within the mountains. (The agency lists the trails' conditions as between "fair" and "not maintained" and places limits on the size of groups on the trail.) I first hiked into the wilderness in 1970. Even then the trail was busy with visitors. The wilderness includes a huge portion of the associated volcanic field that extends many miles east and northwest of the landmark mountain. The range is a hodgepodge of ash beds, volcanic tuff, and old lavas dissected by time, but everywhere abounding with rich vegetation of the Sonoran Desert. Some of the volcanics appear to have continuity with Picketpost Mountain to the southeast. The high point of the range is 5,059 feet (1,542 m), roughly 4,000 feet above the city of Phoenix.

According to most geologists, the mountain we see from the south and west is the remnant of a massive caldera that exploded around 25 MYA, part of the Oligocene-Miocene volcanism that shook southern Arizona for a few million years. After the bottom blew out of the volcano, ejecting its contents for hundreds of miles in all directions, it collapsed, forming a caldera. Gradually the magma chamber filled again and swelled the ground in the middle of the caldera, producing what is known as a resurgent dome. What we see today are the eroded remnants of that dome. The sides of the caldera have been removed by millions of years of attacks by rain, wind, and heat.

Numerous gated communities circumscribe the southern and western periphery of the Superstition Mountains, limiting access and photographic possibilities. Access to some trails, however, remains available and worthwhile. The state of Arizona maintains Lost Dutchman State Park near Apache Junction.

Table Top Mountain, from Interstate 8 west of Casa Grande.

Table Top Mountain
INTERSTATE 8, WEST OF CASA GRANDE

From the east, especially along Interstate 8 west of Casa Grande, Table Top is hard to miss. It sits a couple of miles south of I-8 and viewed from the east its top appears to be as flat as a table. And, at an elevation of 4,373 feet (1,333 m), it rises more than 2,000 feet from its base. Viewed from other directions, however, its outline loses the similarity to a table and its summit appears more irregular and undulating, which it is. The O'odham call it Mo'ochbaḍ, a noun meaning "the top of one's head."

The peak is the principal feature of the Table Top Wilderness, which is contained within the boundaries of Sonoran Desert National Monument. The latter encompasses a huge swath of Sonoran Desert both north and south of I-8. This unit, administered by the Bureau of Land Management, was established in 1990 to afford a measure of protection for the Sonoran Desert and its vegetation, which has been steadily encroached on by development of one sort or another over the last century. The area also has a history of small-scale mining of copper, gold, and silver.

The vegetation receiving protection around Table Top is a rich gathering of Sonoran Desert plants. Well represented are saguaro cactus, foothills palo verde, and the ironwood tree, with a healthy sprinkling of cactus species, a wealth of shrubs and herbs, and, along washes, mesquite trees. This vegetation supports a variety of wildlife that belies the land's arid appearance. Lizards, snakes (including several species of rattlesnakes), a host of bird species, arthropods, and small and large mammals, including coyotes, badgers, bobcats, occasional mountain lions, and even bighorn sheep thrive in this supposedly barren environment. The vegetation at the summit of Table Top is grassland with a mix of higher-elevation plants quite different from those at the base.

Access to the peak is via the Vekol Valley exit on I-8. In recent years the valley has become a popular route for those traveling on foot from south of the border without the documents required by the U.S. government. Some of these folks are rumored to be smugglers. Parts of the valley are strewn with items cast aside by those attempting to find refuge and anonymity and perhaps markets in urban areas. Most visitors from the United States are far more likely to encounter white and green U.S. Border Patrol vehicles, aircraft, and personnel, who may subject such citizens to interrogation.

Table Top's top is of volcanic origin, as is the case with most of the mountains nearby. The volcanic cap is about 23 million years old—early Miocene. The volcanic matter spewed from the summit covers very old rock—1.7-billion-year-old Pinal Schist and 1.4-billion-year-old Oracle Granite—that composes most of the mountain and is the origin of alluvial sediments along its base and in its washes. The mountain's general shape is a result of Basin and Range block faulting.

Texas Canyon boulders, part of the Little Dragoon Mountains, seen from Interstate 10.

Texas Canyon, Little Dragoon Mountains

INTERSTATE 10, BETWEEN BENSON AND WILLCOX

The unusual mountain of rocks named the Little Dragoon Mountains forms the backdrop for the highest and most interesting point on Interstate 10—all 2,460 miles of it. The high point sits at just under one mile above sea level. The canyon, in reality a pass, lies to the southeast of the interstate highway as it passes through the mass of boulders. Texas Canyon separates the Dragoon Mountains to the south and the Little Dragoon Mountains to the north. The freeway is carved from the south side of the Little Dragoons, which rise to just over 6,500 feet (about 1,985 m). The Arizona Department of Transportation wisely located rest stops on each side of I-10 among the towering boulders of the canyon. The majesty of the surrounding formations often causes visitors to delay their departure. The gigantic rock formations formed from granite, not the higher peaks, make this place a landmark.

Texas Canyon forms a corridor for wildlife and for humans, ancient and modern. Just prior to the Civil War the Butterfield Overland Mail Company forged a short-lived stagecoach route through Texas Canyon following a trail that had existed for centuries. The Southern Pacific Railroad also followed the route, which is the most direct from the eastern United States to Tucson and hence to Yuma, on the Colorado River, and Southern California. The first trains passed through in 1883. Currently, most of Texas Canyon is private ranchlands or Arizona State Trust lands that are fenced and closed to the public. Use permits can be obtained through the Arizona State Land Department. Holders of valid Arizona hunting licenses in pursuit of game have legal access to most state lands.

This area has affinities with the Dragoon Mountains to the south, but the Little Dragoons form a geologically separate range. Like the Dragoons, Texas Canyon was a favorite of Apaches, who found the vast field of boulders and glades of oaks much to their liking. The mountains provided an abundance of agaves and acorns, prime food sources, and convenient nooks for shelter and easy places to hide from enemies.

Texas Canyon shares with the Dragoon Mountains a vast display of colossal and rounded boulders that climb the hillsides. However, the ages of the two plutonic bodies differ greatly. The granite of Texas Canyon (more appropriately classified as quartz monzonite) has been dated at roughly 52 million years old, of Eocene times. The granites of the Dragoons are mostly younger—20 to 25 million years old, of Oligocene-Miocene times. The Little Dragoons are far more geologically complex than the neighboring Dragoons. They demonstrate outcrops of Pinal Schist, the 1.7-billion-year-old base of much of southern Arizona. In addition to the Precambrian schist, a variety of Paleozoic and Mesozoic rocks are represented. The range is also heavily mineralized, and a large body of copper ore underlies much of the southeast side of the range, including the right-of-way of I-10.

The massive, roundish boulders of Texas Canyon were originally magma, molten material derived from the earth's mantle. During the Laramide orogeny a large blob of it pushed toward the surface, forcing its way upward and raising the surface many thousands of feet above the magma chamber. The magma never reached the surface. Pressure from below lessened, and the enormous mass began to cool and solidify, a process that may take millions of years. During the slow cooling crystals formed, mostly of feldspar, a silicate mineral that on cooling results in grains large enough to produce a rough surface. That coarse texture gives climbers plenty of traction on boulders and combined with their roundness makes them a delight to clamber over.

Granite is especially subject to foliation or flaking, as it disintegrates underground and at the surface. In this slow process sheets, rather than chunks, flake off, often circular pieces. If sufficient rainwater (but not too much) penetrates the soils, the carbon dioxide dissolved in it forms a weak acid that attacks feldspar, gradually turning it into clay. As the acidic water seeps into cracks and joints of the buried granite, it slowly dissolves the surface. Because sharp corners have the most exposed surface area, the rainwater dissolves them quickest, slowly rounding them as they shed layers, until they are so rounded that they have no more edges. As surface erosion— mostly rain and wind—excavates the granite such as that found here in Texas Canyon, the rock sooner or later emerges as rounded boulders surrounded by decomposed granite and clay. And it beckons to climbers. If rainfall is lacking or excessive, granite outcrops will not become rounded. Over the last 50 million years or so, Texas Canyon has received just the right amount of rainfall.

Thumb Butte, Prescott National Forest.

Thumb Butte

PRESCOTT

For those who lived within Prescott city limits in the mid-twentieth century, Thumb Butte was a daily reminder and an orientation point. It loomed over the western end of town, as familiar as a cathedral. It has been a civic landmark since the town was Arizona's capital city— for three years, 1864–67. Since the 1960s, Prescott has expanded far beyond its original location in a northeast-facing valley, from most parts of which Thumb Butte is visible.

Now, as the city has spilled out over ridges and basins, many Prescottonians view the landmark only occasionally, if at all. Pity. It juts up from the forested highlands all by itself. Its summit, at about 6,500 feet (1,981 m) sits roughly 1,200 feet above Whiskey Row at the city's center. Several trails lead to the top, but those on the butte itself are closed to the public for part of the year, usually from February through mid-July, during nesting season for the peregrine falcons that find the lofty lavas much to their liking. A public park and picnic area at Thumb Butte's base are heavily used. From there roads depart into the forests of Prescott National Forest in several directions. Mountain bikers abound.

The landmark is part of the Sierra Prieta, which includes Granite Mountain to the north. The other peaks in the range are of ancient granite. Thumb Butte's looming dark presence contrasts handsomely with the sea of light brownish to yellowish granite country rock that juts up throughout the region. The peak is the lone volcanic presence around Prescott.

Thumb Butte is a newcomer in an ancient land. The granite that surrounds its lavas is of Proterozoic vintage, in the vicinity of 1.7 billion years old, while the butte's rock, basaltic lava, is a mere 14.5 *million* years of age, making it of mid-Miocene origin. A slug of magma, derived from a large body that lay beneath much of the Prescott region, somehow found a weak spot in the granite and poked through, producing a lava flow that we see today as Thumb Butte. Many popular accounts consider the mountain a volcanic plug, similar to Agathla, but more recent investigations suggest it is merely the remnant of a large basaltic flow that has maintained its elevation for our benefit while the less resistant volcanic material has been eroded away. When Thumb Butte is viewed from the south, its resemblance to a thumb becomes more apparent than it is from downtown Prescott.

The principal spine of the Tucson Mountains seen from downtown Tucson. Wasson Peak at 4,687-feet elevation is at the far right.

Tucson Mountains

TUCSON

The craggy Tucson Mountains, named after the modest metropolis to the east, provide a dramatic backdrop for the west side of Tucson. The Tucson Mountain District of Saguaro National Park occupies much of the northern portion of the range, while Pima County's Tucson Mountain Park contains much of the southern portion of the mountains. The highest point is Wasson Peak at elevation 4,687 feet (1,428 m). It rises roughly 2,500 feet above the channel of the Santa Cruz River, where sediments 10,000 feet deep obscure the lower rock of the range.

Wasson Peak lies within the boundaries of Saguaro National Park. A popular trail leads to its summit. Several roadways penetrate the range, but only two—Gates Pass Road toward the south and Picture Rocks Road to the north—fully cross the range. An ample parking lot at Gates Pass is often host to geology students hoping to untangle the complexities of the range's creation.

It is also widely visited at sunset, offering sensational views of the mountain ranges one after another, reaching fifty miles to the west. A network of trails nearby provides splendid access to the heart of the mountain.

The Tucson Mountains can be considered the heart of the Sonoran Desert. They contain the world's finest forests of saguaro cactus, as well as the Arizona-Sonora Desert Museum. The area has been home to Hohokam peoples, their ancestors, and their descendants for at least three thousand years, probably much longer. Saguaro fruits constituted a vital part of their diet, in addition to the corn and beans they cultivated on the valley floors and on terraces above the Santa Cruz.

The geological history of the range differs dramatically from that of the Santa Catalina Mountains to the northeast and the Rincon Mountains to the east. Those ranges are both metamorphic core complexes, based largely on Precambrian granitic rock. Much of the rock of the Tucson Mountains is of volcanic material of far more recent origin. While the rock of the Catalinas and Rincons mostly has a relatively smooth surface, that of the Tucson Mountains has been shaken, twisted, lifted, dropped, broken, and stirred so much that geologists refer to it as the Tucson Mountain Chaos. The surface rock is usually quite rough and jumbled, often jagged. Most of the volcanic rock is aged around 70 million years, called Cat Mountain Tuff, referring to a prominence at the southwest side of the range. Occasional office building-sized blocks of limestone of Mississippian age (roughly 350 million years old) appear scattered throughout the range. They are probably fragments of a layer of limestone that was blown into the sky when a massive volcano blew through the limestone, which is a resilient rock. The aftermath of that eruption, when colossal volumes of rock and volcanic matter were ejected, produced a caldera, perhaps twenty miles in diameter. Not long after, geologically speaking, the bottom of the caldera collapsed. With a little help from geologists, visitors can detect the caldera's presence to the west of Gates Pass.

Many geologists who have studied the area believe the volcanic mass originated far to the east, across the Santa Cruz River, atop the Santa Catalina and Rincon Mountains blocks. According to this theory, around 30 MYA a period of intense stretching occurred in the Southwest. As the land was stretched farther and farther, the entire Tucson Mountains block broke off along a low-angled fault known as a detachment fault. Over roughly 13 million years the entire mass slid to the southwest, ferried along by the ever-stretching terrane, as the main body of the Catalinas moved away from it. The volcanic mass came to rest in more or less its present location. During Basin and Range, that is, the last 15 million years or so, further stretching produced faults in the mountains, resulting in great blocks that rotated as their centers of gravity came to rest. During the migration southwestward, the mass of mountains included in the detachment fault were subjected to unruly violence and were broken into untold millions of individual blocks, boulders, cobbles, and stones. The blocks of limestone were carried along and scattered here and there among the upheaved landscape.

Geologists long despaired of piecing together the geological history of the mountains. Only in the later twentieth century did plausible descriptions of the mountains' origins coalesce.

Vermilion Cliffs at Lees Ferry, Colorado River.

Vermilion Cliffs

U.S. 89A, NORTHERN ARIZONA

The Vermilion Cliffs provide an unforgettable backdrop for river
runners about to venture through the Grand Canyon and for travelers
connecting between Flagstaff and Kanab, Utah, via the Kaibab Plateau.
They tower above the northern and western side of the Colorado
River at Lees Ferry. Until the construction of the Navajo Bridge in
Marble Canyon in 1929 just a few miles downstream, that tiny location marked the sole crossing of the Grand Canyon region for more
than three hundred miles.

Lees Ferry is still the embarkation point for river trips. The Vermilion Cliffs rise dramatically above the river at the ferry, only to be
hidden from view by the walls of Marble Canyon once the boat has

departed. For motorists who cross westbound over the Navajo Bridge on U.S. 89, the cliffs tower over the north side of the road for more than thirty miles in a most dramatic fashion. In the nineteenth and much of the twentieth century, U.S. 89A, which crosses the bench beneath the cliffs, was the only practical route from Flagstaff north into Utah. It reached Kanab via the Kaibab Plateau to the west. The construction of Glen Canyon Dam created a much faster route.

From House Rock Valley, where U.S. 89A passes below, the Vermilion Cliffs rise between 2,500 and 3,000 feet, from just over 4,000-feet elevation to just over 7,000 feet (roughly 2,350 m). U.S. 89A skirts the base of the cliffs for about thirty miles before rising into the Kaibab Plateau and hence north to Fredonia and Utah. The cliffs form the southern edge of the expansive Paria Plateau, one of the stepping-stones on the "staircase" of geological formations—a series of ever higher or lower plateaus in southern Utah and northern Arizona. That remarkable array reveals a succession of older to younger layers of sedimentary rock that culminate at Bryce Canyon National Park in Utah.

The cliffs are included in Vermilion Cliffs National Monument, which was established by President Clinton in 2000 and includes much of the Paria Plateau and the sensational multilayered, varicolored formation known as The Wave. Trails crisscross the plateau, but trail permits from the Bureau of Land Management are required and waiting lists are long.

From the cliffs' summit a vast territory appears. Fifty years ago, the San Francisco Peaks, a hundred miles to the south, were usually clearly visible from the rim. But now smoggy air from power plants and other pollutants, some of it from as far away as Los Angeles and Phoenix, have made clear days the exception.

The steepness and inaccessibility of the high cliffs and the yawning view they provide have proved ideal locations for the reintroduction of the California condor. These enormous birds can usually be spotted soaring around the cliffs, searching for meat of dead animals. Many condors have suffered from lead poisoning after ingesting carrion from deer carcasses containing lead shot left behind by hunters. Efforts by wildlife officials to require lead shot to be replaced by nontoxic copper have met with irate resistance from prominent hunting lobbies.

The cliffs are an excellent example of rock strata laid down over hundreds of millions of years and preserved in the order in which they were placed. The varicolored aprons at the base of the sheer cliffs comprise mounding, smooth hills of Triassic age Chinle Formation. Their color and texture are similar to the Painted Desert formations found in Petrified Forest National Park, where the same Chinle Formation provides the color. The Chinle here includes a base of durable Shinarump Conglomerate, a tough layer of sandstone that forms a ledge over the mudstone conglomerates of the layer beneath, the sloping Moenkopi Formation, also Triassic. The Moenkopi in turn rests on Permian Kaibab Limestone, of Paleozoic age, the highest formation of the Grand Canyon. Upward, above the Chinle, are colorful, layered, sometimes blocky cliffs of Jurassic Moenave mudstone and siltstone. (To the east that same formation is called Wingate. I don't know why.) Next above are the sheer cliffs of purple/red Kayenta Formation, primarily sandstone, which at times ends in a distinct plateau at the top. Above that terrace lie the sheer cliffs of pink and whitish Navajo Sandstone, at times continuous with the Kayenta Formation. These three cliff-forming layers are collectively referred to as the Glen Canyon Group, since they are on display in the same sequence throughout Glen Canyon and elsewhere. The formations vary in color, both because of the chemical variability, primarily iron, and the very different physical origins of the formations. Navajo Sandstone forms the soaring cliffs in Zion National Park, a hundred miles to the northwest.

Whetstone Mountains from the east.

Whetstone Mountains

INTERSTATE 10, COCHISE COUNTY

At the intersection of Interstate 10 and Arizona Route 90 between Benson and Tucson, the Whetstones are the compact mountain range to the southwest. The mountains are named for a localized deposit of hard stone called chert, also known as flint, which has been sought after for centuries for making arrow and spear heads and, later, for sharpening knives and other tools. The Whetstones are hardly a huge range, for the highest point, Apache Peak, is only 7,771 feet (2,369 m) in elevation.

Much of the Whetstones' mass is a jumble of strata of differing ages and compositions. However, this geological hodgepodge contains a complete sequence of Paleozoic sedimentary rocks. The strata may be tilted, but they are the most visible and intact sequence in southern Arizona, from youngest to oldest in descending order. This clear record of deep history makes the range an important resource for studying the geological history of southern Arizona. One of those sequences, a thick layer of limestone (in which the chert is embedded), figures prominently in recent Arizona history.

As you view the range from the north or east, the limestone ridges are prominent, especially the Mississippian Escabrosa Limestone, about 350 million years old, more or less contemporaneous with Redwall Limestone of the Grand Canyon and the Harquahala Mountains. Seeing this formation back in the early 1970s and knowing that limestone strata often gave birth to caverns led two cave explorers, one of them a geologist, to suspect the existence of a cave. They had been energized especially after old miners suggested to them that there was a cave somewhere in the region. After careful exploration and surreptitious hiking on private land, they discovered a hole from which warm, moist air was blowing. They labored furiously at nighttime to widen the opening until it was big enough that one of them could squeeze through. In the process, they discovered what would come to be called Kartchner Caverns.

Randy Tufts, a geologist and a co-discoverer, was a friend of mine. He and Gary Tenen proceeded to explore the caverns, discovering grottos and lengthy passages of incomparable beauty, and hoped to acquire the site themselves. That proved impossible; so they informed the rancher who owned the property that he was sitting on a pristine cavern of the first order. Over the next twenty-five years the state of Arizona acquired the site from the Kartchner family and developed it into a state park, now the crown jewel of Arizona's State Parks system. The cave is a marvel of geological diversity, containing formations seen nowhere else, but it is also a rich repository of microorganisms, many of them new to science, that now attract as many scientists as does the geological layout.

To this day I must salute Randy, who went on to gain a PhD in geology. He died in 2002 of a rare disease. Randy was a first-rate cave explorer, but an even greater humanitarian.

Geological Time Classifications

Since the early nineteenth century, geologists have used the combination of fossils and the relative horizontal position of rocks to establish comparative ages of rock strata: younger rock was always deposited on top of older rock; fossils in lower layers were older than those in higher layers. While later events might twist, fold, and upturn the layers, their deposition was always younger on top of older. Where the fossils showed a dramatic change in number or species from one layer to the next, geologists proposed the end of a geological era or period and the beginning of another. Where the fossil record depicted the abrupt disappearance of a broad range of creatures, they saw a mass extinction.

The cause of the extinctions or the burgeoning of new species is still debated, but research has narrowed the candidates. Currently the leading candidate for the cause of mass extinction is cataclysmic volcanic activity, mostly catastrophic outpourings of lava known as flood basalts. Such terrestrial trauma includes the Siberian Traps (250 MYA), the Shatsky Basalts, which lie under the northwest Pacific Ocean (144–147 MYA), and the Deccan Traps of India (66

MYA). Other suggested causes of extinctions include meteor collisions with Earth (corresponding with the sudden mass extinction of dinosaurs at the end of the Cretaceous period, roughly 66 MYA), abrupt and vast releases of methane or carbon dioxide, rapid climatic change such as glaciation or glacial melting, and rapid heating, cooling, drying, or wetting of the earth's climate, often proposed as the cause of Ordovician-Silurian extinctions. Geologists have attributed the burgeoning of new species or the rapid expansion of populations to the advent of more favorable climates or seas more receptive to marine life. The causes of vast amounts of new life and forms have not received the attention given to mass extinctions.

Geologists have developed ingenious and meticulously documented explanations of the geological history of our planet and others. For example, limestone, an abundant sedimentary rock formed from the remains of marine creatures, often demonstrates discernible layers of varying thickness and differing composition. Geologists interpret this as a record of the transgression and regression of seas, oceanic or inland, mostly salt, but occasionally freshwater bodies. Massive deposits and cliffs of sandstone (rock derived from sand) are the heritage of arid climates with marching sand dunes or ancient shallow seas that accumulated vast bodies of sand. Mudstones are the heritage of shallow bodies of water or streams sluggish enough to accumulate thicknesses of mud. Geologists traced many geological formations to the rise and fall of mountain ranges, the forces produced by faults, and aggregation of materials eroded from higher to lower elevations by gravity and weathering. They detected and followed faults, breaks in the earth's crust, tracing how and in what direction each side moved from its former connection and what that meant for the landscape.

Early geologists attached labels to layers or groupings of layers. Most of these names for geological divisions remain with us, a tribute to the scrupulous work of the early geologists. They long ago subdivided each period or epoch into multiple subperiods, which are not mentioned here but are familiar to structural geologists, those who study the layout of the earth. The dates used below are approximate only. They have been highly refined in geological literature, and more precise dating is constantly emerging, incorporating technology of breathtaking sophistication. Some dates remain controversial due to the difficulty of obtaining accurate dates from certain kinds of rock, especially sandstone. The correct dates for boundaries between periods of the Mesozoic era—Triassic, Jurassic, and Cretaceous—are still being debated.

EONS, ERAS, AND EPOCHS (PERIODS)

PRECAMBRIAN ERA   Also referred to as the Proterozoic eon. All earthly time before about 541 MYA, more or less 4 billion years in length. Precambrian life, which goes back at least two billion years, consisted of plants without vascular tissue, bacteria, fungi, and animals without bones or anything hard enough to be fossilized. In Arizona, Precambrian rock is exposed on the surface in multiple locations in the Transition Zone and throughout the Basin and Range Province. It is abundant in metamorphic core complexes such as the Santa Catalina and Rincon Mountains, the Pinaleños, and the Harquahalas. The granites exposed in the Prescott area are also Precambrian, as are the colorful formations of the Salt River Canyon. Rock of such age is not exposed in the Colorado Plateau except where it has been exhumed in the depths of the Grand Canyon. The Precambrian era ends when hard-shelled marine creatures appear in the fossil record, the earliest fossils easily recognized by early geologists.

PHANEROZOIC EON   541 MYA to the present.

PALEOZOIC ERA   About 541–248 MYA. This is the time when marine organisms and, in the later stages, fishes dominated the oceans, but terrestrial life had not yet appeared. It began with an explosion of new life forms, including vertebrates. Most of the rock layers of the Grand Canyon visible from the rim are of Paleozoic age or older. None are younger, except for basalts, including some of Quaternary age, in the western portion, lavas that flowed over the North Rim and plugged up the Colorado River. All other younger rock in the Grand Canyon, that is, rock deposited after the Paleozoic era, has been eroded away.

CAMBRIAN PERIOD 545–490 MYA. Marine animals such as shellfish appeared, and biodiversity exploded. Creatures with bones and shells became common but were confined to oceans. The first vertebrates appeared around 525 MYA. In the Grand Canyon, the Tonto Group (Tapeats Sandstone, which underlies Bright Angel Shale, which underlies Muav Limestone) is of Cambrian age. The era ended when a natural catastrophe eliminated vast numbers of marine species. The cause of this mass extinction is controversial. One prominent theory posits rapid glaciation, which cooled the seas, where most life forms had evolved in warm-water conditions.

ORDOVICIAN PERIOD 490–443 MYA. This era began warm, but cooled rapidly. Fish appeared. The end of the Ordovician is marked by mass extinctions—roughly 60 percent of the world's species disappeared. Glaciers covered much of the earth, and the dramatic change in water chemistry has been the favored theory for the end of the era. More recent investigations point to enormous outpourings of lava as well. Geological material from Ordovician times is remarkably absent from the Colorado Plateau, nor does it appear elsewhere in Arizona except for a few outcroppings in the far southeastern part of the state.

SILURIAN PERIOD 443–417 MYA. Following the extinctions at the Ordovician-Silurian boundary, the earth warmed considerably and there was a burst of new life forms as sea levels rose and warmed. A few fishes appeared, and shallow reef systems became common.

Land plants first appeared. Mass extinctions of a broad range of organisms did not bring an end to the period, but an abrupt change in species makeup appears to define the boundary between the Silurian and Devonian periods. Silurian sediments are also absent from the Grand Canyon and the Colorado Plateau and, for that matter, from Arizona.

DEVONIAN PERIOD 417–354 MYA. New forms of animal life appeared, including amphibians and insects. Fishes abounded, and plants and insects appeared on land. Roughly 75 percent of all life forms on the earth disappeared in the Devonian extinctions. Marine organisms were especially hard hit. What caused the extinctions remains controversial, but the oceans became anoxic, that is, devoid of oxygen, and marine life changed drastically. An unspecified outpouring of basalts may have contributed to the change in oceans and terrestrial climates as well. Some researchers now suggest that there was no general extinction, just a huge shift in the number and nature of the earth's organisms. The Devonian sedimentary record in the Colorado Plateau and in the Grand Canyon is only marginally represented and is scarce in the remainder of Arizona.

CARBONIFEROUS PERIOD 354–299 MYA. The Carboniferous is usually divided in North America into Mississippian and Pennsylvanian periods. Both periods were characterized by tropical climates and thick vegetation, with extremely high sea levels. Mississippian Redwall Limestone forms massive cliffs in the Colorado Plateau and is present throughout much of the western portions of the state and as far south as the Gran Desierto of northwestern Sonora, Mexico. Escabrosa Limestone, clearly revealed in the Whetstone and Mule Mountains of southeastern Arizona, derives from the same period. Thick seams of coal formed from massive swamps during the Pennsylvanian. Reptiles appear in the fossil record. Seas rose and fell numerous times. Toward the end of the period the climates cooled rapidly and much of the earth's surface became covered with deserts. Much of the Supai

Formation in the Grand Canyon is of Pennsylvanian age. The transition from the Pennsylvanian (Carboniferous) to the Permian period is usually defined by widespread alteration of fossil species composition, rather than a catastrophic terrestrial event.

PERMIAN PERIOD   299–252 MYA. Seas covered much of the Southwest. The Permian Kaibab Formation (primarily Kaibab Limestone) forms the cap layer of the Grand Canyon and represents the youngest rocks present in the Grand Canyon sequence. Below it (and the underlying Toroweap Formation) lies Coconino Sandstone, the thick, cliff-forming, light-colored formation well defined in the Grand Canyon and the Mogollon Rim. The underlying Hermit Formation, which features crumbly, slope-forming, relatively soft sediments—the bane of canyon hikers—is also of Permian times. The towering cliffs of De Chelly Sandstone of northeastern Arizona are of Permian times.

The end of the Permian period is defined by mass extinctions on an unprecedented scale. Over 90 percent of marine species disappeared, and more than 70 percent of terrestrial species vanished. The extinctions appear to have been brought on by the global effects of enormous outpourings of basalts in Siberia, known as the Siberian Traps. It took the earth more than 30 million years to recover a semblance of our planet's biological diversity that existed prior to the Permian extinctions.

MESOZOIC ERA   About 252–65 MYA. This is often thought of as the age of reptiles, the era when dinosaurs evolved, the largest terrestrial creatures that ever roamed the earth. The Mesozoic also ends with the rapid disappearance of dinosaurs.

TRIASSIC PERIOD   252–200 MYA. The Triassic was ushered in by extinctions and departed with extinctions. The climate was dry for much of the period. Red beds of mudstone gave a typical sheen and color to many Triassic rock formations. Mass extinctions at the Triassic-Jurassic boundary reduced the earth's species count by 75 percent, but dinosaurs survived and went on to proliferate, perhaps occupying niches newly freed when organisms were wiped out. The extinctions may have resulted from the tearing apart of the supercontinent Pangaea, when the rifting of continents away from the landmass produced massive outpourings of basalts accompanied by colossal volumes of carbon dioxide, which drastically altered the earth's climate. The colorfully banded Chinle Formation is of Triassic origin. Its soft slopes are most notably seen in Petrified Forest National Park, at the base of Agathla Peak, and at the base of the Vermilion Cliffs.

JURASSIC PERIOD 200–147 MYA. The diversity of dinosaur species exploded. In the Southwest, dry climates produced enormous sand dunes, while meandering rivers deposited muds and silts. The splendid Navajo Sandstone cliffs of Zion National Park and De Chelly Sandstone of northeastern Arizona are of Jurassic age. Worldwide, many lush, tropical forests supported the great reptiles. Geologists disagree as to the source of the transition to the Cretaceous, but the emplacement of Shatsky basalts, now beneath the northwest Pacific Ocean, is a likely candidate. The undersea plateau resulting from the massive eruptions is roughly the size of the state of California, and the Tamu Massif shield volcano, which erupted 147 MYA and is a part of the Shatsky Rise, is the largest volcano on the earth, even though its eruptions appear to have been confined to the seabed. The impact of meteorites and enormous tsunamis are both plausible alternative explanations.

CRETACEOUS PERIOD 175–66 MYA. The lengthy Cretaceous period featured abundant reptile speciation and further evolution of the great dinosaurs. Flowering plants appeared. It ended abruptly with the extinction of most dinosaurs along with roughly 80 percent of the world's animal species. Avian dinosaurs survived the extinctions and evolved into birds. Most scientists attribute the extinctions to the Chicxulub meteorite that struck near the Yucatán Peninsula. Others point to the flood basalts of the Deccan Traps of India, a catastrophic outpouring of lava that would have altered the earth's climate for millions of years. At any rate, nearly all the dinosaurs vanished over the next million years or so following the end of the Cretaceous. The Cat Mountain Tuff of the Tucson Mountains is of Cretaceous age.

CENOZOIC ERA 66–2.5 MYA. Also known as the Tertiary era. This is the age of mammals. The boundary between the Cretaceous and the Tertiary is usually referred to as the K-T boundary, with a sharply defined fossil record. Many geologists now divide the Cenozoic era into two parts: the Paleogene period, 65–23 MYA, and the Neogene period, 23–2.5 MYA, and refer to the next layer of divisions as *epochs*, not *periods*. The boundary with the Cretaceous is now referred to as the K-Pg boundary.

The separation of the periods is based on the rapid evolution of mammals, especially primates, birds, and grasses at the beginning of the Miocene. In many classifications the Cenozoic ends at the Pleistocene era, 2.5 MYA, the time when periods of glaciation began. Note also that the Cretaceous period is of longer duration than the entire Cenozoic era. Much, but not all, of the volcanic activity in Arizona that is still visible occurred during the Cenozoic era.

PALEOGENE PERIOD 65–23 MYA.

PALEOCENE PERIOD (EPOCH) 65–56 MYA. The Paleocene started off cool and dry but warmed dramatically. The climate change may be responsible for the die-off of many marine creatures and abrupt changes in the makeup of terrestrial animal species. The Indian subcontinent slammed into Asia and began the uplift of the Himalayas, which disrupted oceanic circulation and may have initiated the warmer climates of the Eocene that followed. The transition to the Eocene and the rapid changes in the fossil record of plants and animals is widely attributed to rapid warming of the earth—between five and eight degrees Celsius—in a matter of a few thousand years. Ocean temperatures rose even more rapidly, and the warming of the seas was even greater than on land. The temperature rise was accompanied by a threefold to fourfold increase in carbon dioxide, a notorious greenhouse gas. A similar effect of rapid warming may be occurring today in permafrost regions of Siberia experiencing enormous exhalations of methane and carbon dioxide. What caused the rapid warming in the Paleocene is controversial, but widespread and continuing volcanic activity and outpourings of basalts in the North Atlantic, known as the North Atlantic Igneous Province, seem to be implicated. This massive outpouring of lava covered much of northeastern Ireland and northwestern England and reached eastward into Norway and westward into Greenland. The eruptions caused the release of untold millions of tons of carbon dioxide.

EOCENE PERIOD (EPOCH) 56–35 MYA. This was a hot and humid time on the earth. In Florissant Fossil Beds National Monument in Colorado numerous plant fossils from the Eocene reveal a tropical climate wholly different from the present. The cause of a wave of extinctions, especially affecting marine organisms, at the Eocene-Oligocene boundary is not clear, but some geologists now believe it may have been a huge meteorite, called the Popigai, that crashed into Siberia, resulting in worldwide climatic disruptions.

OLIGOCENE PERIOD (EPOCH) 35–23 MYA. The Oligocene began with dramatic cooling from the hot Earth of the Eocene. Though the Oligocene was not a cold epoch, the cooling resulted in a broad proliferation of both mammal and plant species, some of them establishing their present habitats. In the U.S. Southwest and the Sierra Madre Occidental in Mexico, it was a time of explosive volcanism that lasted for millions of years. The close of the Oligocene also marks the end of the Paleogene period. The first ice sheets in Antarctica also appeared around the time of the E-O boundary. Researchers increasingly believe the transition to the Miocene is connected to the disruption of ocean currents accompanying opening and closing of seaways due to tectonic movement of continents. Southern Arizona experienced a long period of intense volcanic activity beginning in the late Oligocene and extending well into the Miocene.

NEOGENE PERIOD 23–2.5 MYA

MIOCENE PERIOD (EPOCH) 23–5 MYA. The initiation of the Miocene marks the beginning of the Neogene period. No single event has gained acceptance as accounting for the abrupt change in fossil life, but the Miocene saw the rapid spread of grasslands and the general establishment of vegetative habitats as we now see them. The current climates of the southwestern United States and northwestern Mexico appear to have been established during the late Miocene. In the Southwest, volcanism that began in the early Oligocene continued, and Basin and Range faulting changed the landscape dramatically. The climates were warm compared with those of the Oligocene that preceded the Miocene and the Pliocene that followed.

PLIOCENE PERIOD (EPOCH) 5–2.5 MYA. The Pliocene period is characterized by marked cooling from the Miocene. Although no specific terrestrial event has been identified as the cause of the transition to the Miocene, geological strata and fossils show a sharp change at the boundary. The transition to the Pleistocene is represented by strong cooling and the beginning of modern glaciation.

PLEISTOCENE PERIOD (EPOCH) 2.5 MYA to the present. Also called the Quaternary period. The relatively cool Pliocene gave way to the age of glacier advance and retreat, at least eleven of them, beginning about 2.5 MYA. Some geologists consider the Pleistocene to have ended about 11,000 years ago with the retreat of the Wisconsin ice sheet, our latest glacial climate. We will see.

Some paleoecologists, who study ancient climates and plant-animal interactions, note a wave of extinctions, especially affecting large herbivores and their predators, that occurred around 10,000 years ago. Others suggest we have entered into a new geological period, the Anthropocene, characterized by rapid global heating and a blast of new extinctions, both related to human activity.

Glossary

ANDESITE   Lava whose iron and silicate content lies intermediate between rhyolite (high silicate) and basalt (high iron); it is the most common lava found in the Andes, from which its name is derived.

ANTICLINE   A large rising fold in stratified rock, caused by compression and often severely eroded at the summit, leaving slopes where older layers lie higher than younger layers.

BASALT   Lava rich in iron, usually runnier than rhyolitic lava and more prone to produce lava flows than explosive eruptions.

BASIN AND RANGE   The geological landscape of the southwestern United States and northwestern Mexico produced by extensional stretching of the earth's crust as the North American and Pacific Plates pull apart. Blocks of crust break off as the stretching occurs. Some rise, while those adjacent fall, producing alternating mountains and basins, mostly oriented in a southeast to northwest direction.

BATHOLITH   A large regional deposit or intrusion of magma that has cooled below the surface, forming granite and its close relatives.

BLOCK FAULTING   The separation of a large block of faulted country rock, that is, the basic rock of a region, from the remaining mass due to extensional stretching or compression.

BRECCIA   Rock made up of fragments, often large, cemented into a hardened mixture.

CALDERA   A large crater remaining after a major volcanic explosion.

COMPRESSION   Folding or breaking of rock as plates collide.

COUNTRY ROCK   Rock native to an area.

DESERT VARNISH   The shiny patina that develops on rock surfaces in hot, sunny, and arid regions. Just how it forms remains controversial.

DETACHMENT FAULT   A low-angled fault in which a large section of a land mass "detaches" from the rock beneath and "slides" off. Detachment faults are associated with regions that have undergone extensional stretching and mountain ranges demonstrating metamorphic cores.

DIATREME   A tube through which magma reaches the surface. The remnant volcanic rock in Agathla Peak is evidence of an ancient diatreme.

DIKE   A solidified magma that has forced its way vertically through layers of country rock (rock native to an area) of a different composition; often associated with diatremes.

EXTENSIONAL STRETCHING   A thinning of the earth's crust as plates move apart in opposite or lateral directions.

FAULT   A widespread fracture in rock that displaces one side in relation to the other side.

GEOLOGICAL TIME   Expressed by geologists as (1) eons, the lengthiest sequences, for example, Phanerozoic; (2) eras, the highest category of sequences within an eon, for example, Paleozoic, Mesozoic; (3) epochs (also referred to as periods), highest category within an era, for example, Cambrian, Miocene.

GNEISS Metamorphic rock formed from igneous or sedimentary primary rock subjected to great heat and pressure. In metamorphic core complexes, gneiss is primarily derived from granite deep below the surface.

GRABEN A large block faulted away or broken off from the surrounding rock and sinking below the surface.

GRANITE Igneous rock of high silica content, primarily feldspar and quartz, formed when magma pushes toward the earth's surface without breaking through and then cools at the site.

HOODOO Rock eroded to form strange vertical formations.

HORST A large block faulted away from the surrounding rock and rising above the surface, associated with and opposed to a graben, which falls.

HOTSPOT (VOLCANIC) A specific region of upsurge and breakthrough of magma and volcanism unrelated to plate boundaries. Plates move over the hotspots and magma punches through to produce volcanoes as the movement occurs. Examples are the Galapagos Islands, the Hawaiian Islands, and the Yellowstone National Park region.

IGNEOUS ROCK Rocks derived from magma or volcanic activity, mostly lavas and various forms of granite.

LACCOLITH A mountain produced by an upwelling of magma mushrooming and forcing the surface to swell upward without the magma breaking through.

LARAMIDE OROGENY The great mountain-building period of the late Cretaceous to the mid-Eocene, 80–40 MYA, which created many of the mountain ranges in the interior western United States, especially the Rocky Mountains; it resulted from the low-angled subduction of the Farallon Plate eastward under the North American Plate, tectonic activity that reached as far east as the Black Hills of South Dakota and northeastern Wyoming.

LAVA Magma that reaches the earth's surface in flowing or explosive form.

LIMESTONE A sedimentary rock formed by accumulation of former marine or lake creatures or their leavings, cemented together by chemical processes and pressure.

MAGMA Molten rock material confined by planetary crust.

METAMORPHIC CORE COMPLEX A mountain range where tectonic forces have caused a surface rock mass to detach and slide off, relieving pressure from the metamorphic rock below the fault, allowing it to rise toward or above the surface.

METAMORPHIC ROCK Rock whose physical structure has been altered by heat and pressure.

MONOCLINE A fold in the surface of a widespread rock layer where subterranean forces caused one side of a fault to drop or be elevated and the overlying layers bend upward or downward.

MYLONITE, MYLONIC SHEAR Mylonite is a hard volcanic rock produced by shear when faults move against each other; it is commonly associated with detachment faults in which an upper layer of great dimensions slides off the layer below. Mylonic shear is the deformation of the mylonite that appears as smears or stretches.

OBSIDIAN Volcanic glass, formed when lava cools quickly, preventing crystals from developing.

PLATE TECTONICS The dynamics of the earth's crust created by the collision, separation, and lateral friction among the various plates that cover the earth's surface. Relief (topography) on the earth is a result of (1) plate collision (the Himalayas), (2) subduction (one plate diving under another such as in the Andes), (3) place divergence or rifting (the Gulf of California), (4) lateral (sideways) bumping (San Andreas Fault), or (5) hotspots, magma forcing its way to the surface as a plate passes over a point of weakness in the crust.

PLUTON   A local ballooning upward of magma that has cooled and solidified into granite and its close relatives but has not reached the surface.

PYROCLASTIC FLOW   A large mass of superheated volcanic ash, rock fragments, and gases that emerges from a volcanic eruption and flows downward into the volcano's surroundings.

QUARTZITE   A very durable metamorphic rock derived from sandstone subjected to intense heat and pressure.

RHYOLITE   Lava with a high content of silicates. Rhyolite tends to emerge from below the crust as a thicker liquid and is more subject to explosive volcanic activity than basalt.

SANDSTONE   A sedimentary rock created by sand, whether from sand dunes, river-deposited sands, or ocean-derived sands, cemented together by chemistry and pressure, often mixed with mud or silt.

SCHIST   Platy metamorphic rock that results from layers of (mostly sedimentary) rock subjected to intense heat and pressure. Often derived from mudstones or shale, which are in turn derived from muddy sediments of lakes or river deltas. Mica is often derived from schist.

SEDIMENTARY ROCK   Rock created by an accumulation of sediments, primarily limestone, sandstone, mudstone, and shale and mixtures of them.

SILL   Solidified magma that has forced its way horizontally through passages in country rock (base rock of a region) of a different composition. Sills may be many hundreds of feet thick.

SPREADING CENTER   The zone along which tectonic plates diverge or pull apart, creating a rift zone. Spreading centers are frequent sites of volcanic activity.

SUBDUCTION   The penetration of one tectonic plate beneath another.

SUBDUCTION ZONE   The region between where a burrowing plate dives under the overlying plate and where it disappears into the earth's mantle. The zone may be hundreds of miles wide and thousands of miles long.

SYNCLINE   A large downward fold in stratified rock caused by compression and often severely eroded on the sides, where older layers lie above younger layers. Often found alongside anticlines.

TEPHRA   Volcanic material that has fallen to earth composed of ash and small rock fragments.

TUFF   See *volcanic tuff*.

UNCOMFORMITY   The placement of one geological stratum above another that has eroded away over long periods of time such that significant amounts of the geological record are missing between the layers.

VOLCANIC TUFF   Rock resulting from compacting and welding of volcanic ash into harder rock.

Index

About the Author

David Yetman is a research social scientist at the Southwest Center of the University of Arizona. His research has focused on peoples and plants of the Sonoran Desert region. His books include *The Great Cacti: Ethnobotany and Biogeography* and *The Organ Pipe Cactus*. He is producer and host of the PBS television series *In the Americas with David Yetman.*

The Southwest Center Series
Jeffrey M. Banister, Editor

Ignaz Pfefferkorn, *Sonora: A Description of the Province*

Carl Lumholtz, *New Trails in Mexico*

Buford Pickens, *The Missions of Northern Sonora: A 1935 Field Documentation*

Gary Paul Nabhan, editor, *Counting Sheep: Twenty Ways of Seeing Desert Bighorn*

Eileen Oktavec, *Answered Prayers: Miracles and Milagros Along the Border*

Curtis M. Hinsley and David R. Wilcox, editors, *Frank Hamilton Cushing and the Hemenway Southwestern Archaeological Expedition, 1886–1889*, volume 1: *The Southwest in the American Imagination: The Writings of Sylvester Baxter, 1881–1899*

Lawrence J. Taylor and Maeve Hickey, *The Road to Mexico*

Donna J. Guy and Thomas E. Sheridan, editors, *Contested Ground: Comparative Frontiers on the Northern and Southern Edges of the Spanish Empire*

Julian D. Hayden, *The Sierra Pinacate*

Paul S. Martin, David Yetman, Mark Fishbein, Phil Jenkins, Thomas R. Van Devender, and Rebecca K. Wilson, editors, *Gentry's Rio Mayo Plants: The Tropical Deciduous Forest and Environs of Northwest Mexico*

W. J. McGee, *Trails to Tiburón: The 1894 and 1895 Field Diaries of W J McGee*, transcribed by Hazel McFeely Fontana, annotated and with an introduction by Bernard L. Fontana

Richard Stephen Felger, *Flora of the Gran Desierto and Río Colorado of Northwestern Mexico*

Donald Bahr, editor, *O'odham Creation and Related Events: As Told to Ruth Benedict in 1927 in Prose, Oratory, and Song by the Pimas William Blackwater, Thomas Vanyiko, Clara Ahiel, William Stevens, Oliver Wellington, and Kisto*

Dan L. Fischer, *Early Southwest Ornithologists, 1528–1900*

Thomas Bowen, editor, *Backcountry Pilot: Flying Adventures with Ike Russell*

Federico José María Ronstadt, *Borderman: Memoirs of Federico José María Ronstadt, edited by Edward F. Ronstadt*

Curtis M. Hinsley and David R. Wilcox, editors, *Frank Hamilton Cushing and the Hemenway Southwestern Archaeological Expedition, 1886–1889*, volume 2: *The Lost Itinerary of Frank Hamilton Cushing*

Neil Goodwin, *Like a Brother: Grenville Goodwin's Apache Years, 1928–1939*